1966

GENERAL METAPHYSICS

JOHN P. NOONAN, S.J.

GENERAL METAPHYSICS

LOYOLA UNIVERSITY PRESS *Chicago*

Imprimi Potest:
William J. Schmidt, S.J.
Provincial of the Chicago Province
April 4, 1956

Nihil Obstat:
Austin G. Schmidt, S.J.
Censor Deputatus
October 23, 1956

Imprimatur:
✠ Samuel Cardinal Stritch
Archbishop of Chicago
October 24, 1956

Printed in the United States of America
Library of Congress Catalog Card Number: 57-6669
P-POLA-PE-OE

"The end of philosophy is not that we may know

what men have thought

but what the truth of things is."

St. Thomas Aquinas:
I *De coelo et mundo,* Lectio 22.

PREFACE

THE purpose of the author in writing another textbook on general metaphysics in English is to clarify and simplify as far as possible the basic ideas of philosophy. Without a reasonably complete and intelligible course in ontology the rest of philosophy loses its unity and consistency and is not nearly so helpful or interesting to the student.

Too much reliance has been placed in the past on Latin textbooks which were written mostly for courses in seminaries. Philosophy today is being taught to an ever-widening and more diversified group. In view of this all the matter that is mainly theological has been eliminated from the present book. An attempt has been made to express the ideas in idiomatic English instead of the literal Latin-English so commonly found. The purpose throughout has been to bring the matter within the comprehension of the average undergraduate and thus to provide him with the background of knowledge so necessary for other courses of philosophy.

The author makes no apology for his eclecticism, and thinks none is needed. He yields to no one in his appreciation and reverence for the great minds of the past, but he considers that they have left much to be done by men of the present and future, that the last word has not yet been said and in fact never will be said as long as man exists. There are many important philosophical problems still remaining unsolved. In speaking of Aristotle as "the philosopher," the scholastics almost universally were impressed by his arguments and not by his authority. We see no reason for having any different attitude toward the scholastic philosophers themselves, whether for one of them or for all of them. Much remains to be done, and it will never be accomplished by excessive and undiscerning adulation of one man or group of men.

This is a textbook on philosophy; it makes no attempt, according to the motto of St. Thomas on page v, to decide about disputed texts or varying interpretations of history. All such material is outside the scope of a book for undergraduates, which has as its purpose to develop an understanding of basic principles. Our hope is that those who are now learning the fundamental "truth of things" will one day be so far advanced as to engage in these learned discussions with profit.

J. P. N.

CONTENTS

GENERAL METAPHYSICS

CHAPTER I

THE PURPOSE AND IMPORTANCE OF METAPHYSICS

WE know from experience that the mind of man is constantly reaching out for more and more knowledge, just as his will is ever desirous of more and more love. The search for knowledge varies with the individual, but the race of men has always carried on the quest in accordance with its nature and for the practical and speculative value that knowledge brings with it. The advance in knowledge in modern times fairly staggers the mind and leaves it struggling and helpless in the vast sea of truth. But that knowledge has been mostly of one kind, of material things, to such an extent that the investigation of anything that is not helpful and practical for the material side of life has fallen into disuse and derision. Some modern scientists regard with contempt all efforts to pierce the veil of matter which surrounds us and to rise to heights of thought more in accord with man's spiritual nature. For them there is only one kind of science, empirical or experimental; for them nothing is true except what can be proved in a laboratory by the test of sense experience. All that is not material is in their opinion unknowable, and indeed even the material is, so they think, known only by its appearances, its real nature being a mystery which human minds cannot possibly pierce.

If their contention were true, there could of course be no philosophy, much less that branch of it called metaphysics or ontology. That it is not true is proved in other branches of philosophy. There is no reason why there cannot be a science of ultimate reality any more than there is a reason why there cannot be a science of proximate reality. If the individual sciences can become such by reduction of their results to order and system, so can man arrange the principles of a higher science which will underlie and support them all.

Philosophy, then, is a real science albeit not an experimental one. It investigates and classifies the common elements in all science in an effort to arrive at a higher unity and synthesis of knowledge. The individual sciences investigate the *proximate* causes of things; philosophy, on the other hand, is the science which studies things in their *ultimate* causes, employing human reason alone. It goes beyond the data of the special sciences and endeavors to find the reasons and principles which underlie these sciences and which scientists often assume without examination or proof. It is the task of philosophy, and especially of the highest branch of philosophy, which is known as "first philosophy," general metaphysics, or ontology, to investigate and prove the principles that are assumed in the lower sciences. This investigation of philosophical problems is especially important inasmuch as many scientists have fallen into error because they assumed the truth of principles which had never been proved and which were actually false.

The term metaphysics was originally used to indicate that part of the works of Aristotle which came "after the *Physics*" or the study of nature in the concrete. It had originally only the signification of the location the study occupied in the books of Aristotle. In the course of time, however, it came to signify that branch of knowledge which was above and beyond physics because of its investigation of ultimate reality. It is a most apt phrase to describe the discussion of reality in its most fundamental aspects and has been used in that signification by practically all philosophers. Metaphysics, then, may be defined as the science of the ultimate principles and properties of real things. In the words of Suarez: "Metaphysics has for its purpose to show forth the nature, properties, and causes of being as such, and of the divisions of being inasmuch as these divisions prescind from material conditions."[1] It is, then, properly spoken of as the science of "being as being" since it considers being in itself, without regard to whether the being is material or immaterial, actual or possible, real or logical.

Metaphysics is divided into two sections, general metaphysics or ontology and special metaphysics. Special metaphysics is subdivided into three parts: cosmology treats of the general nature of the world; psychology studies the nature of man as a being endowed with reason; and the-

[1] *Disputationes metaphysicae,* I. All translations are the author's unless an English edition of the work is indicated.

odicy or natural theology considers the nature and attributes of God.

Ontology

A science is a body of truths, arranged and ordered by rational analysis of evident or agreed upon facts. It is the knowledge of things in their causes. Empirical sciences look for the proximate causes of things, whereas philosophy seeks to know ultimate causes.

The definition of any particular science gives its material and formal objects. By material object is meant the general subject of study of the science. By formal object is meant the particular phase or aspect under which the general subject is regarded and by which one science is distinguished from other sciences which have the same material object. Man is the material object of a number of different sciences. The science of anatomy studies man's structural make-up; the science of physiology studies the functions of the organs and parts of man's body; the science of psychology treats of the mind and soul of man. Thus these sciences are alike in their material object (man) but they differ in their formal objects, since they consider man under different aspects.

Ontology is the science of being in its most general aspects. The material object of ontology, then, is being: being as opposed to nothing or nonbeing and including that which is or can be, the actual being and the possible being. All other sciences also treat of being, but being of some particular kind. Ontology studies being in its most general aspects, and in that we have its formal object. Things as they are found in nature must be either material or immaterial; however, the science of ontology does not consider them from either of these aspects but rather under the general features which are common to both and which are attributes or determinations of being in general or being as such. Consider the general divisions which are found in the table of contents, notions such as essence, existence, substance, accident, quality, relation, cause, and the like. They cover every sort of being, material or immaterial. They go beyond mere physical qualities, such as weight, heat, light, or color, and must be considered metaphysical properties of being as such. The investigation of these deeper attributes of reality, then, must be considered as separate from the physical sciences. It is a science in its own right, with its own formal object and its own methods of investigating the truth of things.

Importance of metaphysics and ontology

We have already mentioned the attitude of modern science, and indeed of the modern mind, toward philosophy in general and metaphysics in particular. It might be well to illustrate this point by giving a practical example.

Several years ago Mortimer Adler, a scholastic philosopher, was invited to deliver a series of lectures before the Institute for Psychoanalysis in Chicago. It soon became apparent that Professor Adler's views were diametrically opposed to those of his audience. After the lecture series was completed Professor Adler decided to publish his material in book form and to invite Dr. Franz Alexander, director of the Institute for Psychoanalysis and a leading exponent of the antimetaphysical point of view, to write an introduction in which he would be free to state his own position. A few excerpts from that introduction by Dr. Alexander will serve to indicate the type of opposition that the philosopher must meet today.

> During these discussions it became evident that our disagreement represents two diametrically opposite points of view, and illustrates the unsurmountable gap between what could be called a scientific *Weltanschaung* and the dogmatic attitude of a Thirteenth Century scholastic. . . . This contempt for "practical" accomplishments explains why he [Mr. Adler] considers the futile speculations and meditations about human nature of ancient and medieval philosophers like Aristotle and Thomas Aquinas to be superior to our detailed and precise knowledge of normal and pathological mental processes which enable us to influence these processes in a desired direction and thus cure mental ailments (p. xi).
>
> In view of this incomplete nature of science, only two attitudes remain for a human being in handling his desire to orient himself in the world in which he lives: a. A kind of agnosticism, contenting himself with the answers which science can offer at any given time, abandoning the wish for an integrated concept of the universe. b. An attempt to integrate the isolated and disconnected answers of science into a *Weltbild*. This is philosophy (p. xii).
>
> The psychoanalyst considers the difference between man and animals as definitely of quantitative nature because he can observe that the new-born infant shows no human but merely animal characteristics. The difference between men and animals, which is one of Adler's fundamental theses, comes gradually about during the individual's development from an ovum to an adult (p. xiv).
>
> If there is such a thing as turning back the clock of history and science, here we see a classical example of it. Scho-

> lasticism, a sterile form of deductive thinking, developed as a harmless outlet for the reasoning powers of man in a period of intellectual servitude when man could not observe the world around himself lest any observation come in contradiction with prevailing dogmas. He had to content himself with flawless deductions from incorrect premises. Free observation of facts was forbidden; rigid acceptance of preconceived ideas was the highest requisite (p. xvi).[2]

These are the views of Dr. Franz Alexander, head of the Institute for Psychoanalysis. It is hard to believe with how much contempt and ridicule some scientists regard the idea of the attainment of knowledge by intellectual activity, and it might be well to read that entire introduction or some similar statement which can be found in many of the books of modern science, especially those on psychology and psychiatry. Unless we understand the attitude of our opponents we will be inclined to be slack in our defense of truth. It is obvious that such an opinion is hostile not only to philosophy, but to religion and morality as well, and that it threatens the foundations of civilized society.

This disposition of mind has been called scientism because for men who have such an attitude the empirical sciences alone have any value as sources of knowledge. It must be admitted that marvelous results have been obtained by modern methods of experimentation in the sweeping advances of our knowledge of the material world. It is unfortunate that some scientists have been led by this success to the conclusion that their own special

[2] Mortimer J. Adler, *What Man Has Made of Man,* pp. ix-xvi. New York: Longmans, Green and Company, 1937.

kind of knowledge is the only kind worth while, and that all other knowledge is merely opinion or sentiment. The dangers of such an advance in material knowledge without a corresponding deepening of intellectual and moral values is so obvious and has already received so much notice that it needs no further comment.

The state of mind of such scientists is based upon a misinterpretation of the nature of philosophy. Philosophers do not deny any of the facts discovered by real science. They gladly accept them and try to fit them into their proper places in a higher system. Metaphysics is the basis of all true science. The concepts treated in ontology, such as substance, quality, relation, cause and effect, are fundamental to all truth and to all scientific knowledge of whatever kind. There should be, then, no conflict between physical science and the science of ontology.

Is it true, as experimental scientists pretend, that they disregard metaphysics in their investigations? The opposite is the fact. They must meet these notions wherever they turn; and in their ignorance of philosophical disciplines they come to the wrong conclusions about them, thereby undermining the whole realm of truth and endangering the real good of mankind. It is evident, therefore, that ontology is a science of fundamental importance for every aspect of human knowledge and human life.

Methods used in ontology

The charge is often made that philosophy, and especially metaphysics, is built up without any regard to experience and observation. This charge is manifestly untrue.

The philosopher accepts all the proved facts from the physical sciences and acknowledges the authority of each science in its proper field. He also uses the inductive method in his own field.

The main source of truth and certitude in philosophy is natural knowledge resulting from the experience of mankind through many centuries of thought. Upon this are built both the natural sciences and the science of philosophy. These facts of experience give rise by analysis to the principles and concepts which are the foundation of metaphysics and of all philosophy. In philosophy the deductive method is used primarily for the discovery of new truths and principles which by the power of the mind can be drawn from the results of experience, observation, and experimental research. It is through philosophy, and especially through metaphysics, that the sciences can be furnished with a solid foundation of knowledge, the known truth and validity of the fundamental ideas upon which they are all based. Philosophy without science is sterile; science without philosophy is unsound and irrational—it is scientism.

Sources of a sound metaphysics

The *Metaphysics* of Aristotle is the chief source of a sound philosophical system. In this and the other works of the Stagirite are found the true answers to most fundamental questions, in spite of the fact that physical science was in his time still in its infancy and full of gross errors and childish fancies. The works of Plato are also worthy of close attention, particularly because it is almost impossible to understand Aristotle without an acquaintance with Plato. Then come the great masters of the Middle Ages, Thomas Aquinas, Albertus Magnus, Bonaventure, and John Duns Scotus. Aristotle is spoken of by them almost universally as *the* philosopher, on whom they relied to support their opinions. References to the works of these men may be found in the bibliography.

Our analyses are based also on the works of the great commentators of St. Thomas, as his were on the works of Aristotle and Plato. Among them are Scotus, Suarez, Cajetan, John of St. Thomas, Vasquez, and a host of others. In particular the solutions found in the text are in agreement with the contemporary Latin works of Hontheim and Frick. Many are beginning to realize, however, that truth is not to be found in sterile commentaries on the past but in the clash of controversy with contemporary thought with a view to the development of fresh approaches. It is not a simple or easy road by which one makes his way to the eternal.

SUMMARY OF CHAPTER I

1 The nature of man is such that he must seek after truth, the meaning of the world about him, and the laws and causes of all things.
2 Science is the knowledge of things in their causes. The empirical sciences look only for proximate causes. Philosophy seeks the ultimate causes of all things, using human reason. All sciences are complementary and not hostile to one another.
3 Metaphysics is the science of the ultimate principles and properties of real beings. General metaphysics, or ontology,

treats of being in general. There are three branches of special metaphysics: cosmology treats of the material world; psychology of the soul of man; theodicy, or natural theology, of God.

4 Ontology is the science of being in its most general aspects, of being as being. It investigates such realities as being, substance, accident, essence, existence, relation, quality, cause and effect.

5 The importance of ontology may be seen from the enumeration of the realities above mentioned. These realities are the foundation for all science. Unless science accepts and understands them it is irrational; it becomes scientism.

6 Ontology uses both the inductive and the deductive method, though the latter particularly distinguishes it from physical science. Its main sources are the works of Aristotle as explained and interpreted by the great thinkers of the Middle Ages.

CHAPTER II

THE CONCEPT OF BEING

THE term *being* has two senses, a participial one and a substantive one. In its participial form, the present participle of the verb *to be,* it means *existing.* As a verb *to be* is not always used in this sense; it may also be used as a mere copula to unite two ideas, prescinding altogether from actual existence. In its substantive form the noun *being* does not imply actual existence but merely a relation to existence; that is, it refers to whatever does exist or can exist, the existible.

When we speak of a being in the concrete the word has the same meaning as *thing* and includes everything that we know: persons, places, facts, and phenomena of whatsoever kind. It is used in the same sense as reality in the concrete sense. Whatever is real is a being or thing, and whatever is a being is real in some sense.

The idea of being resembles a universal idea, especially in that it can be either direct or reflex. We form the direct idea of being in somewhat the same way as we form the direct universal, using the abstractive power of the mind; we form the reflex idea of being and the reflex universal by the reflective power of the mind, by what St. Thomas calls an act of "second intention."

The direct concept of being

Everything which our senses report to us is a being of some kind. Our parents, our house, our dog, and everything connected with them are all beings. They are indeed beings of a particular kind but they all have one feature in common: they are actually existing things, and we can and do think of them as such. They are all very different among themselves, but the mind can turn its attention to the common element only that it finds in them and forget all the distinguishing marks; in doing so it forms the idea of being, thing, reality.

As we mentioned previously, the term *being* applies also to things which are only capable of existence, which have possible existence rather than actual existence. This is the philosophical and ontological meaning of being as the word is used by Aristotle throughout his works, and especially in the *Metaphysics*. He calls possible being "incomplete" being as opposed to the "complete" being of the actually existing thing; incomplete being is nevertheless being, as opposed to *nothing* or *nonbeing*. All the men and things which will come into existence in the future are now possible beings; they have a relation, a reference to existence, a capacity for existence. They are real beings; they are not nothing.

There are, then, as we shall see more fully presently, two kinds of real being, the actual and the possible; or, as we shall call them in more scientific terminology, the physical and the metaphysical.[1] Both are real beings. An actual being is a real being in the full and complete sense, since it not only could exist but actually does exist. A possible being is a real being in what we might call an incomplete and partial sense. While it does not exist here and now, it is not merely nothing; it could have complete being; it is a possible being and has a positive essence in opposition to nothing, which has no essence and can never exist in the world of reality.

Formation of the idea of being

In order to determine exactly how the mind forms a concept of being, it is necessary to make at least a brief analysis of the mental processes of abstraction and precision. Abstraction is an act of the mind whereby it fixes its attention upon one characteristic of a thing or upon one element common to many things, excluding other elements which are joined to it in the real order. Precision is a form of abstraction in which the mind represents one idea apart from others with which it is really identified. There are two different kinds of precision, objective and

[1] In connection with this use of the words *physical* and *metaphysical* it is essential to remember that physical in this sense is not a synonym for *material*. Physical being includes all existing things, material or immaterial; trees, plants, dogs, men, angels, and God are all included when we speak of physical being. Physical as it is used here means the same as *actual, really existing*. Metaphysical being, on the other hand, includes possible being and also ideas or concepts, which are objectively possibles.

subjective.[2] When the idea that is represented is objectively different from the other ideas with which it is identified in the physical order (as, for example, the idea of animal is objectively different from the idea of rational) the precision is called objective. When the ideas are only subjectively different, when they include each other implicitly, the precision is called subjective.

The best examples of objective precision are found in the Porphyrian tree, the arrangement by Porphyry of the metaphysical grades of being of Aristotle. We submit on page 16 this famous old diagram as an aid to the discussion and place the idea of being in what, for the present, may be considered its proper position.

It is apparent from the diagram that, according to Aristotle, man is a rational, sentient, living (organic), material (corporeal) substance (reading up the left side of the diagram). In order to give a strict definition according to genus and species, this may be shortened to "Man is a rational animal." Are all these ideas in the definition of man objectively different or subjectively different? They will be objectively different if they have a different thought content, or essence, or comprehension, so that one idea does not necessarily include the other. The ideas will be only subjectively different if they include each

[2] It may be well to remark that various terminologies are used by different authors here as well as in a hundred other places. It is best to adhere to one. Subjective precision is also called formal or logical precision; objective precision may be called material or metaphysical. If you are confronted with these other terms in other places, remember that they were called objective and subjective when you first met them. This warning applies in general to many of the terms used in ontology. Holding fast to one set of terms or, as an alternative, recalling the various sets, will do much to simplify the study.

other implicitly although they do not expressly mention each other.

Let us examine a few of these ideas. In the brief definition of man as a rational animal does the idea *animal* in-

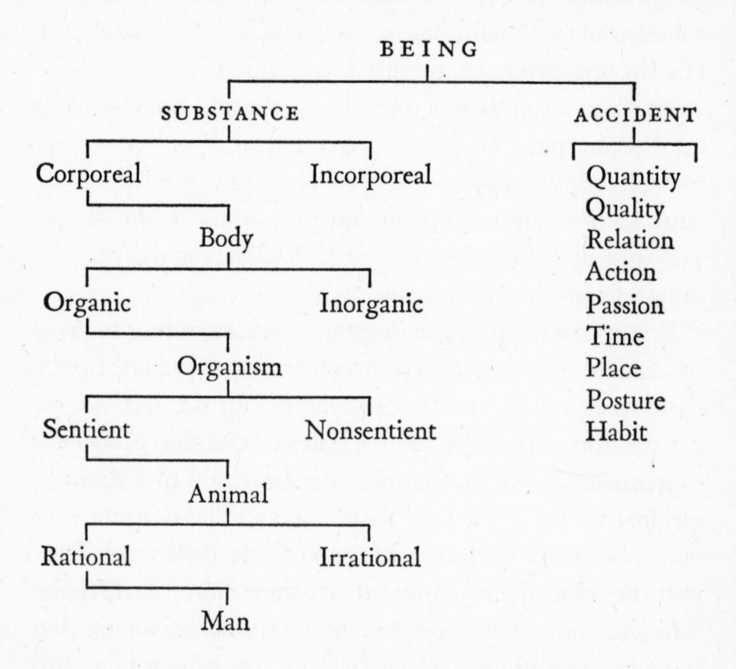

clude the idea *rational?* Obviously not, for the idea *animal* can be verified in beings which are not rational and, on the contrary, the idea *rational* can be verified in things which are not animal. The idea *animal* is not the same as the idea *rational*. These two ideas are concepts that are objectively different. Therefore when these ideas are abstracted from man's essence, the process is one of objective precision.

The same thing is also true of the other branches on the Porphyrian tree. *Sentient* means something that is capable of sense perception; it does not include the idea *rational,* for brute animals (dogs, horses, and so forth) are sentient but not rational. The idea *living* or *organic* means capable of immanent activity; it does not include the idea *sentient,* for plants are living but do not have sense perception like animals. And so on for the other concepts—each has its own thought content or essence, even though in man they are all found together. These ideas do not include each other implicitly. They are objectively different, and the mind arrives at them by an objective precision.

When we compare these ideas with the idea of *being* at the top of the diagram we perceive that there is a great difference. All these ideas contain within themselves implicitly the idea of being, and the idea of being contains every one of these ideas implicitly because being includes every kind of reality. The idea of being, therefore, includes them all and is included in them all implicitly, although they do not expressly or explicitly mention each other. The precision of the idea of being, then, is only subjective because the difference between the two concepts is only subjective. For example, in one case the mind produces a more general or obscure idea, *being*. In another case it produces a clear idea, *substance*. The difference, as has already been said, is merely subjective. The action of the mind in producing a clear concept or an obscure concept of the same reality may be compared to a man looking at a ship approaching from far out at sea. At first it is only a spot on the horizon, then it becomes clearer and clearer, and finally it is recognizable as a ship, his own ship, having such and such characteristics. There is no change in the thing itself; it has received only a subjective determination. So it is with the eye of the mind. The idea of *being* includes all other ideas or essences, and all other ideas likewise include *being;* everything is a being and being is everything. The precision of the idea of being, therefore, is a subjective precision.

The reflex concept of being

Just as a universal idea can become reflex by an act of second intention of the mind, so the transcendental idea, *being,* can become reflex by the same sort of act; that is, the mind may compare the direct concept, *being,* with reality and see that it includes all kinds of beings, thus producing the reflex idea.

The idea of being is evidently the first idea in the logical order—it is the foundation of all other ideas and contains them all implicitly or in a confused and indeterminate manner, not representing them as a certain kind of being but as being in general. Hence the notion of being in general is at the basis of all other ideas, essences, or objects of thought and is the one into which they are all ultimately merged.

The idea of being is also first in the order of time, the chronological order. This fact is not a matter of strict proof, for no one could recall his first idea and what its nature was. Nevertheless it is general knowledge that the mind of man always proceeds from the more confused idea to the more determinate and detailed idea. Now, the idea of being is the most confused and indeterminate of our ideas; therefore it is natural to suppose that it was our first.

In the ontological order, the order of being, the idea of being is not first. God is first in this order, for without God, pure act *(actus purus),* there could be no other being, either actual or possible. In the real order God is and must be first. To confuse the idea of God with the idea of being in general is to fall into pantheism.

The idea of being is the narrowest in comprehension and the widest in extension[3] of all ideas. The comprehension of being embraces only one note, that which is existible, that which is not nothing. Its extension, therefore, is greatest of all, transcendental, extending to or applying to everything that exists or can exist.

SUMMARY OF CHAPTER II

1 The term *being* is derived from the verb *to be.* As a noun it means anything that has or can have existence. The mind forms the idea of being from the things that are represented to it, for they are all beings of some kind. They have a common element, existence, actual or possible; they are existible.

The mind arrives at this idea of being by means of a subjective precision. It is subjective because being includes all other beings, and everything that is existible is a being.

[3] Comprehension and extension were, of course, treated in logic. Comprehension means the total number of notes contained in an idea; extension means the total number of individual things to which the idea extends or applies. Comprehension and extension are obviously in inverse proportion; the greater the comprehension of an idea, the less its extension, and vice versa.

If any distinction is to be made, then, it must be subjective or mental. It cannot be an objective precision because the ideas prescinded are not objectively different from each other as are, for example, the grades of being: rational, sentient, living, and material.

2 **Reflex concept of being.** The idea of being is first in the order of ideas, the logical order; and in the order of time, the chronological order. It is not first in the ontological order, or the order of existing things. God *(actus purus, ens perfectissimum)* is first in this order. The idea of being is narrowest in comprehension and widest in extension.

3 **Definition of being.** No strict metaphysical definition of being is possible because *being* has no genus and no specific difference outside of itself. We therefore give only a descriptive definition, enumerating the two kinds of real being, actual (physical) and possible (metaphysical)—that which exists or can exist.

CHAPTER III

KINDS OF BEING

THERE are many divisions of being. The most important and fundamental division is into the two kinds of real being, actual and possible, physical and metaphysical. To real being is opposed only nothing, nonbeing. The ideas brought out in this chapter will be further elaborated later when we discuss the concepts of potency and act, and especially the idea of possible being. For the present we must try to distinguish what has reality of whatever kind from what has no reality, no being, no matter how it may be called.

Real being

Real being is that which has or can have existence independently of man's mind. It is called real because it does not depend on man's mind for existence. It has a relation to existence which is not connected with man's thought. A being entirely dependent on such thought was called by Aristotle a logical being *(ens rationis)* as opposed to a real being *(ens reale)*.

Both actual and possible being, then, are real being because they have existence or a relation to existence not dependent on man's mind. An actual being is one that really exists here and now in the physical order, the order of existing things. We ourselves are such beings, and everywhere about us in the world of nature are countless other physical beings. They may be visible or invisible, material or spiritual. If they have existence in the present or had existence in the past, they are or were actual, physical beings *(entia physica)*.

A possible or potential being is one that does not actually exist but which is capable of existence. It has an essence, a positive thought content; it is not absolutely nothing; it has some reality, incomplete or partial though it may be. The unborn great granddaughters of James and John are possible beings. They can and may exist at the proper time and given the proper causes. Let us agree to call the being which they now have metaphysical being *(ens metaphysicum)*.

Being and nothing

Nothing is the absence of real being. We can think of it and speak of it only because we have a knowledge of real being to begin with. We acquire the idea of *nothing* by having a knowledge of real being and then denying its presence. The idea of nothing is thus a negative concept. By noting the different ways in which nothing is opposed to various kinds of being, we can distinguish between various kinds of nothing.

An absolute nothing is the total absence of real being, either actual or possible. An example of an absolute nothing would be a square circle or a stick with only one end. These so-called beings contain contradictions in terms. It is absolutely impossible that they could have existence, for one part of the concept cancels out the other. Such concepts are pure mental constructs and have no relation to reality. Since they have neither existence nor the possibility of existence, such "beings" of the mind are really "nothing," although they are, as will be pointed out later, spoken of as logical beings.

A relative nothing is the absence of a particular kind of being. This is further divided into negative and privative relative nothing. A negative nothing is the mere absence in a thing of some kind of being which it would not normally have and which its nature does not call for: the absence of reason in a brute animal, the absence of life in a stone, the absence of feeling in a plant. A privative nothing is the absence in a thing of some kind of being with which nature ordinarily endows it: the absence of feeling in an animal, or life in a plant, or of reason or speech in a man. It is a real privation of something which naturally and normally belongs to the being.

Logical being

There are certain products of thought which have no being except in the mind and which are therefore known as "being of reason" *(entia rationis)*. They are nonbeings, nothings, considered by the mind as beings: *"id quod a ratione excogitatur ut ens, cum tamen in se entitatem non habet*—that which is thought of by the reason as a being, although in itself it does not have any being."[1] Two classes of these logical beings or beings of reason are usually given by authors: one without a foundation in reality, and the other with a foundation in reality.

1. A logical being without a foundation in reality is a pure mental construct. It is the same as the "absolute nothing" mentioned in the preceding section. Examples would be a square circle, a stick with only one end, a corporeal spirit, and similar contradictory concepts. One part in such a dual concept actually denies and removes the reality of the other part, and hence there is no positive reality left. The mind, however, as Suarez says, represents them as if they had a positive thought content and real being.

2. A logical being with a foundation in reality has no real being, actual or possible; however, the mind finds in an existing object a sufficient reason for forming the concept. Logical being with a foundation in reality may be subdivided into three kinds: negative logical being, which is a concept corresponding to negative nothing; privative logical being, which is a concept corresponding to privative nothing; and relative logical being.

A negative logical being is a concept representing a mere absence of a certain kind of being in an object which does not require this kind of being. The concept of sightlessness in a stone and the concept of irrationality in a brute animal would be examples of negative logical being.

[1] Suarez, *Disputationes metaphysicae,* disp. 54, sec. 1, n. 6.

These concepts are negative and can have no being outside the mind; but there does exist some positive reality of which they are negations.

A privative logical being is a concept which represents a lack of being in a thing which ought to have it according to nature. Examples are death, blindness, insensibility. Sightlessness is the mere absence of sight, while blindness is the privation of sight in a being which normally possesses it. Lifelessness is the absence of life in a being to which it does not belong by nature—for instance, in a stone—while death is a privation of life in a being which once had life.

A relative logical being is a concept representing a relation between ideas, judgments, or reasoning processes existing in the mind itself. Relative logical beings are the products of acts of second intention *(actus secundae intentionis)* and therefore have no physical (actual) or metaphysical (possible) being. They have existence only in the mind. Such are, for example, the concepts of genus, species, the reflex universal, and all abstract ideas, such as beauty, truth, holiness. None of these concepts exist or can exist in nature, but they are formed by the mind from its consideration of actually existing things. The relations existing between subject and predicate, between premises and conclusion, between parts of speech, between genera and species, are likewise logical entities which have objective being only in the mind. Such "beings" have a foundation in reality because they are based ultimately on real objects which the mind has known.

From what has been said it is clear that logical being is the same as the *nothing* which has been discussed previously. The definitions and divisions and examples are the same, with one exception. In logical being there is one additional division, relative with a foundation in reality, but it is obvious that a being of such a kind is just as much nothing as any of the other types of nonbeing that have been enumerated. So far, then, we have two kinds of real being, actual and possible (physical and metaphysical); nothing; and logical beings *(entia rationis),* which are the same as nothing.

Ideal being

There is also another kind of being, commonly spoken of as ideal being or intentional being. In general, ideal being may be defined as a being in some way connected with mind, either subjectively or objectively. Ideal or intentional being is divided by all authors into objective ideal being and subjective ideal being. Objective ideal being is the essence or thought content which the mind abstracts from a physical being. Subjective ideal being is the *representation* in the mind of some object of thought; that is, in the act of knowledge the mind actively produces an image of this thought content within itself. This image, this awareness of an object in the mind, this thought presence, is subjective ideal being. The object which is known, of which the mind has this subjective image, is the objective idea or concept, and therefore has objective ideal being.

How is subjective ideal being connected with physical being, metaphysical being, and logical being or nothing? It is connected in this way, that the mind has such images as it may form from all three, since they are all objects of thought, each according to its own nature.

How, in particular, is subjective ideal being connected with the two kinds of real being, physical and metaphysical? There is no doubt that we have ideas of actually existing physical beings. It is also obvious that these physical beings do not come into the mind of themselves, and that the mind has no power to bring them as they are into itself. There must nevertheless be some sort of union between the mind and the thing; otherwise there could be no knowledge. In the act of knowledge, therefore, the physical or actual being receives another form of being, a form of being which the mind can readily embrace. We call this kind of being ideal or intentional being, understanding it now as the thing imaged and not the image of the thing; that is, in its objective aspect and not in its subjective aspect. This is objective ideal being. It is entirely different from the physical being of the object, which it has of its own nature independently of the realm of thought.

Thus objective ideal being is a thought content, an essence, a real being which has its reality independently of the human mind. As such it is identical with possible or metaphysical being, which has reality outside the mind. This matter will become clearer in later chapters, but may be clarified now by the use of the diagram on page 28.

It is clear from the diagram that metaphysical being *(ens metaphysicum)* or objective ideal being is the means of acquiring knowledge of physical being *(ens physicum)*; the mind abstracts the essence of the physical being and thus acquires a knowledge of it. In metaphysical being the essence is already abstracted, and therefore can become of itself an object of rational thought. But it is an essence, a thought content, a positive reality, a possible being, one which can exist.

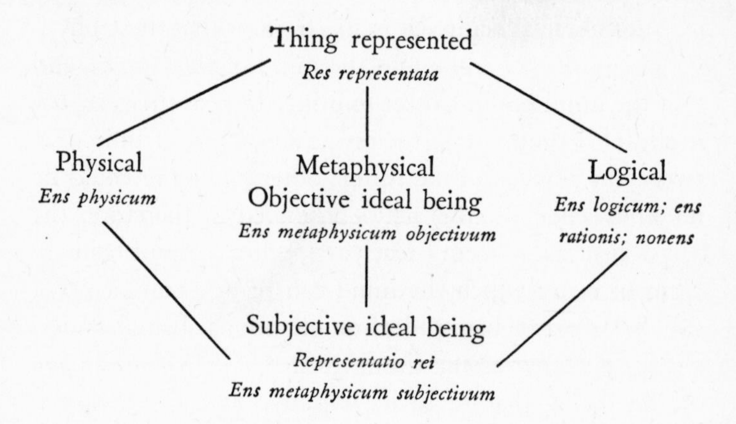

According to St. Thomas a nature or essence may be considered in three ways:

1. According to the being which it has in individuals, where it may be sick, or tall, or white. The individual essence is the essence as it exists in a particular being independently of the action of the mind. It is the sum of all the notes by which the thing is constituted this individual being. "Socrates who is a certain essence is nothing else than animality and rationality which is his essence."[2] This is the *ens physicum* of the diagram.

2. According to the being which it has in the mental state *(in statu logico)*, where it may be called a species or a genus. The universal essence (that is, the essence as ab-

[2] *De ente et essentia*, cap. 2.

stracted from all individuating characteristics) is the specific essence. Concerning it St. Thomas says: "The essence signifies something common to all natures through which different beings are placed in different genera and different species just as humanity is the essence of man and so of others."[3] This is the *ens logicum* or *ens rationis* of the diagram.

3. According to its being absolutely considered in which it may be called animal or rational, although these attributes may belong to it also in the concrete and the abstract state. The essence absolutely considered is the sum of all its perfections or constituent parts, without any regard to whether it is singular or universal.[4] This essence is that which is signified by the definition. This is the *ens metaphysicum objectivum* of the diagram.

Divisions of real being

Thus far we have considered real being as it is divided into physical being and metaphysical being. It is also possible to divide real being in other ways on the basis of its various characteristics. For example, as we have already said, every real being must be either physical or metaphysical—actual or possible; considered from another aspect, every real being must also be either necessary or contingent; it must be either infinite or finite; substantial or accidental; absolute or relative.

Necessary being and contingent being. A being is said to be necessary when its nonexistence is impossible. This

[3] *Ibid.*, cap. 1.
[4] *Ibid.*, cap. 3.

necessity may be absolute or conditional. A being is absolutely necessary when its nonexistence is impossible under all conditions. Such a being must exist, for its existence is identical with its essence. An absolutely necessary being can never be a produced thing; otherwise at some time it would have been merely potential and that would contradict its absolute necessity. Existence is a necessary part of its infinitely perfect essence; it is "being of itself" *(ens a se)*. It is obvious that God and God alone can be such a being. In Him essence is existence; His essence is to exist. Consequently His essence can never be without actual existence; He is the pure act *(actus purus)* of Aristotle.

A being is conditionally or hypothetically necessary when its nonexistence is impossible under certain conditions. Thus, the existence of no man is necessary, but if he exists, he must have the nature of man; he is necessarily a rational animal, and a contingent or unnecessary being. The same is true of all created natures. They do not exist necessarily, but if they exist, they must have their true essence; otherwise they would not be what they are.

A contingent being is one whose nonexistence is possible. It is as such indifferent to existence; it could either exist or not exist as far as its nature is concerned. If it exists, it must be a produced being *(ens ab alio)*, it must have received existence from some other being. If it were not produced by another being, it would owe its existence to its own essence, and it would then be not contingent but necessary.

Infinite being and finite being. A finite being is one which is limited in perfection. Everything in the world is thus limited. It is limited in power, in action, in quality, in time, in space. All our direct and intuitive knowledge is of being which has limits to its perfections. If we have knowledge of the infinite, it is by denying that it is finite —a negative and discursive concept.

An infinite being is one which has no limit to its perfections. While our idea of the infinite is negative in form, it has a positive content in that it affirms the fullness of being and perfection.

A being is actually infinite when it has physical reality without limit. If a being existed in the positive fullness of all perfection, it would be actually infinite. Such a being would possess all perfections, including those that are found in other beings outside of it. It would have to have these perfections in a different manner, in a higher degree *(eminenter)* than they exist in other beings. It is obvious, then, that the actually infinite being must be God, a pure spirit, infinitely perfect, without any kind of potentiality *(actus purus, ens perfectissimum)*. It must be the same as the necessary being *(ens a se)* of which we have just spoken.

A being is potentially infinite when it is without limit in its potentiality for receiving more perfections, though it is always actually limited in the perfection it possesses at any time. Its potentiality is without limit precisely because the source of perfection is infinite, and therefore inexhaustible. The amount of perfection it actually possesses must always remain limited; otherwise it would be an infinite being, and this is incompatible with potentiality.

Substantial being and accidental being. A substance is a being that exists in itself *(ens per se)* and that does not need another being as a subject of inherence. Such are all of the ordinary things that we know through our senses as objects existing in the physical world, such as a desk, a chair, a table, or another human being. They all have their own separate existence and are not mere modifications of some other being.

An accident, as opposed to substance, is a being that cannot exist in itself but requires another in which to exist as in a subject of inherence *(ens in alio)*. As Aristotle points out, there are a great many ways in which one thing may be said to exist in another. Without enumerating them all, we may say that a real accident is in a subject in such a manner that it is not a part, and that it is impossible that it should exist without that in which it is. Accidents, therefore, are essentially modifications of a substance. Such are, for example, the color of the desk (quality), the beauty of the chair (quality), the dimensions of the table (quantity). It is impossible for such things to have being except as modifying and inhering in another, a substance.

Absolute being and relative being. A being is absolute if it can be thought of without reference to another. It is independent of other beings in the order of thought. Such are most ordinary objects, such as table, chair, desk, man, horse, dog. They can be defined or explained in themselves and their meaning is clear as independent units of thought.

A being is relative if it can be thought of only in reference to another. We see this logical relation in ideas such as father, brother, child, friend, similar, equal, and so on. Each of these ideas has a term toward which it looks and to which it refers. There can be no father without a child, and no brother without two children, thus related. A friend implies someone to whom he is friendly.

SUMMARY OF CHAPTER III

1 Real being is anything that has or can have existence independently of man's mind. It includes actual or physical being and possible or metaphysical being. Actual being is that which exists in the physical order. Possible or metaphysical being is that which is capable of existence. It has reality in the metaphysical order. It is the incomplete being of Aristotle.

2 *Nothing* is the absence of being. Absolute nothing is the total absence of being, while relative nothing is the absence of a definite kind of being. A relative nothing is negative when it is the mere absence of being in a thing to which that particular kind of being does not belong by nature; it is privative when it is the absence of being in a thing to which that kind of being does belong by nature.

3 Logical being is anything which has existence only in the mind; it is nonbeing conceived as being *(nonens conceptum ut ens)*. It is the same as *nothing* and has the same definitions and divisions except that it includes a relative logical being, which is a concept representing a relation between ideas or processes existing in the mind itself *(actus secundae intentionis)*.

4 Ideal being is of two kinds, subjective and objective. Subjective ideal being is the picture or image or representation in the mind itself. We can have subjective ideal being of the two kinds of real being and even of nothing or logical being. Objective ideal being is the thing as it is pictured, imaged, or represented by the mind. It is the essence or thought content which the mind abstracts from the physi-

cal being; as such it is identical with the possible or *ens metaphysicum objectivum*.

5 A being is said to be necessary when its nonexistence is impossible. A contingent being is one whose nonexistence is possible.

A finite being is one which is limited in its perfections. An infinite being is one which has unlimited perfection. Being could be actually infinite or only potentially infinite.

A substance is a being which exists in itself. An accident, as opposed to substance, is a being which exists in another, ultimately in a substance.

A being is absolute if it can be thought of without reference to another. A being is relative when it cannot be thought of without reference to another.

CHAPTER IV

ACT AND POTENCY

ONE of the most fundamental of all the primary determinations of being is the division of being into act and potency. All physical reality outside of God is essentially a mixture of becoming and being, of potential and actual. In fact, whether we are examining the constitution of physical being or of metaphysical being, the nature of these concepts of act and potency must be understood before we can proceed very far in our investigations. Historically, the doctrine of act and potency was an outgrowth of Aristotle's attempt to answer the difficulties of the Eleatics and Heraclitus about the nature of becoming. Our discussion of problems connected with the nature of becoming will be reserved for Chapter 6.

As immediate divisions of being the concepts of act and potency are incapable of strict definition, for in a strict definition of them the concept of being would have to be a genus. As has been pointed out previously, being has no genus and is not a genus itself. This makes it impossible for us to give a strict definition, and we must be satisfied with a descriptive definition or explanation.

An act, as opposed to potency, means any entity of whatever kind which perfects a thing in its being. An act is any perfection that belongs to a being, including its own metaphysical being, since that is its first perfection. The term *act* includes the power or faculty (for example, the intellect) as well as the operations or actions of that faculty because both are perfections of the being; it includes every accidental modification of a being because every accident perfects the being in some way (for example, weight, strength, size, and shape are perfections of a man); it includes the essence of a thing because essence is a being's first complete perfection; it also includes the act of existence because existence gives a new perfection to a being.

Potency is the capacity or aptitude for something. It is, of course, the correlative of act: the potency is for an act. A being which is capable of receiving a certain act of perfection is said to be in potency for that act. A few examples may help in understanding the general idea: an acorn has a potency to become an oak tree, an egg has a potency to become a chicken, hydrogen and oxygen have a potency to unite and become water.

The relation between act and potency is one of the completing to the incomplete, the determining to the determinable, the perfecting to the perfectible. It is possible for a being to be an act and a potency at the same time, but under different aspects. It may be a perfection in itself and thus an act, and still be capable of receiving another perfection and therefore be in potency for another act. The intellect and will of man are positive perfections for a man, and thus an act for that man; but they are capable of thinking and willing, and hence in potency for such activities. To say that the intellect and will are both act and potency involves no violation of the principle of contradiction, for the same thing is not affirmed and denied under the same aspect *(sub eodem respectu).*

Kinds of potency

There are various types of potency. First of all, potency may be divided into objective potency and subjective potency. Objective potency is the capacity of a nonexistent being for existence. Though such a being has as yet no actual physical existence, it is not on this account nothing; it has a capacity for existence and hence is a possible, a metaphysical being, a positive entity, which can be given complete being by actual existence. The as yet unborn and unthought-of descendants of the present generation are such beings in the objective metaphysical order. The acorn, the seed, and the egg, which now actually exist and are therefore beings in the physical order, have the capacity to produce the oak, the grain, and the chicken, which are in potency in the objective physical order.

Subjective or physical potency is the capacity of something already existing for another act or perfection. Subjective potency may be subdivided into receptive potency and operative potency. A *receptive* subjective potency is the capacity for receiving something. The mind has a capacity for receiving knowledge. Water has the capacity of becoming ice or steam. An *operative* subjective potency is the capacity for doing something. The mind and the will of man can produce their appropriate acts of thinking and willing, lightning has the power to destroy a home, a bomb has the power to destroy a city.

Possibility or objective potency

Objective potency, the capacity or aptitude of a being for existence, is also called possibility. Impossibility is the incapacity of a being for existence. It is true that only the infinite intelligence can know all that is possible or impossible for the physical universe He has created, but that is not the question here. The question is of metaphysical or absolute possibility or impossibility, and the human mind can discover many of the things that are possible or impossible in this sense. For instance, if a thing actually exists, we know that other things like it could also exist. If James and John were once possible and are now actually existing beings, so the granddaughters of James and John, now only possible, can come into existence in the future by the operation of the proper causes. We also know certain things to be impossible because they violate the principle of contradiction. For example, we understand the nature of a circle and a square, and we know that a square circle is impossible, while a circle larger than the one now before our eyes is quite possible. We know the nature of God and of creatures, and we know that a created God is an impossibility.

Mythology has furnished us with a great number of fanciful conceptions, such as a centaur, a winged horse, an eagle-headed lion. Though such objects do not exist, have not existed, and in all probability never will exist, there is no contradiction in their existence. They are merely physically improbable or impossible, if you will, but they are not metaphysically contradictory.

For a thing to be adequately possible—that is, for it to have the capacity of passing from the state of nonexistence to the state of existence—two things are required and sufficient. The first, as has just been pointed out, is that there be a positive thought content with no contradiction in its notes or terms. This is called the *intrinsic possibility* of a thing. The second requirement for the complete possibility of a being is that there should exist an efficient cause capable of producing it. The men and women capable of producing granddaughters to James and John are in existence, and therefore those granddaughters are possible. So it is with next year's crop of wheat and corn, or next year's production of all kinds of goods, natural and artificial: there are efficient causes capable of bringing these things into existence. This is called the *extrinsic possibility* of a being.

Extrinsic possibility is of two kinds, physical and moral. Physical possibility is that which is possible for any being acting according to the laws of its nature. A man with a cold is physically able to walk a mile to church, and a woman with a small child can leave the child without care and do the same.

Moral possibility, as the term is used in ethics, is concerned with the advisability of following a certain course of action that is physically possible. To say that a thing is morally impossible in this sense means that it is impossible without a greater amount of difficulty or hardship than is required in this particular instance. In other words, it does not mean impossibility at all, but rather an inconvenience which in these circumstances relieves one of responsibility. Thus it might be morally impossible for a man suffering from a heavy cold to go to church, although it would not be physically impossible for him to do so. In the same way, a mother could be excused from her obligation if she had to take care of a sick child.

Moral possibility may also be taken in another sense. When it is said that a certain thing is morally impossible, what may be meant is that with human nature as it is this particular event simply will not occur; it is morally certain that men will act in accordance with their nature. It is physically possible for any normal individual in normal circumstances to avoid any given sin, but it is morally impossible for everyone in a city with a million inhabitants to pass an entire day without even a slight transgression against the law. It is physically possible for a healthy person to pick up a revolver and pull the trigger, but it is morally impossible for normal mothers to shoot their newborn infants. With human nature as it is, such things do not and cannot happen; that is, we have moral certainty that they will not happen. This kind of moral possibility is studied in the science of epistemology.

Reality of the possibles

The reality of possible being has been explained several times in previous pages. From the definition of being with which we started our discussions we saw that what can exist has being, although of a different kind than the being of that which actually does exist. The latter we call physical being, the former metaphysical. Metaphysical being is real being, in spite of the fact that only physical being has full reality. The metaphysical being is not nothing; it has an objective essence or thought content in itself *(in se ipso)*.[1]

The possibles, then, have real, objective being; they are things, they are not no-things. They are capable of existence, whereas *nothing* is absolutely incapable of existence. The possibles have a positive thought content, a real essence; for example, a mountain of gold, a crystal palace (understanding that these beings are not existing, but only possible). *Nothing* has no essence, no reality; it is not an objective idea; it can be known only through the denial of objective being. This can be seen also from the fact that the possibles have real differences among themselves. They are objectively different concepts. Thus a possible man differs from a possible stone; a possible granddaughter, Mary, of one man differs really from a possible granddaughter, Margaret, of another man. Often one possible depends on the eventual existence of another possible as its cause: the existence of Mary and Margaret will depend on the existence of a son or daughter to James

[1] It is to be noted that Aristotle in explaining possible being acknowledges the truth that is found in the doctrine of Plato that ideas are things—not things in the physical order as Plato thought, but in the metaphysical order as Aristotle explained it. To deny that this is the doctrine of Aristotle is to miss the whole point of Aristotelian metaphysics. He even speaks of the possibles as "existing" in the metaphysical order, though for the sake of clarity we shall use the word "existing" only when speaking of the physical order.

or John, who may at the present time be only a possibility. Suarez writes:

> There is the same relation of the possibles among themselves as of things actually existing among themselves, because no things become or exist except those which were formerly possibles. A possible man has no other essence than the one which he will have if he exists.[2]

The potentiality to become an oak is something real in the acorn; if it were not so, if it were nothing real in the acorn, we could say with equal truth that a man, or a horse, or a house is potentially in the acorn; or, again with equal truth, that the oak is potentially in a mustard seed, or a grain of corn, or a pebble, or a drop of water. Therefore the oak is really in the acorn—not actually but potentially. This potentiality in the acorn is subjective or physical, not objective or metaphysical.

There is, then, a real difference among the possibles. Of course it is only a metaphysical real difference, not a physical one; but between "nothing" and "nothing" there is no real difference of any kind. Thus the possibles are positive metaphysical being *(ens metaphysicum objectivum)* just as the direct universals are, as we shall see more fully in a later chapter.

Grounds of possibility

Extrinsic possibility presupposes intrinsic possibility, for no efficient cause can produce a thing the notes or terms of which are contradictory and cannot be realized together. The compatibility of notes is thus an absolute or

[2] *Disputationes metaphysicae,* disp. 6, sec. 3, n. 7.

metaphysical condition; the existence of an adequate efficient cause is a relative condition, for a higher cause might be able to produce a particular being if a lower cause could not do so. The fulfillment of these two conditions is the proximate ground of possibility.

It is also necessary, however, to discover the ultimate ground of possibility, to discover how any possible being is able to have intrinsic and extrinsic possibility. Thus we are seeking the ultimate reason for all possible reality.

Ultimate extrinsic possibility

The ultimate ground of extrinsic possibility consists in the omnipotence of God as guided by His infinite intelligence. It is evident that finite causes do not and cannot produce the total reality of their effects, for that would be creation, and finite beings do not have this power; they can merely change existing reality. They may be true causes, but they are proximate causes. The ultimate efficient cause of possible beings must be infinite, for only an infinite power is capable of producing the potentially infinite number of possible things. But the causality of God proceeds from His omnipotence. Hence that is the ultimate ground of all extrinsic possibility.

Ultimate intrinsic possibility

Intrinsic possibility consists of the compatibility of notes of the possible being. Is this compatibility ultimately due to the possible beings themselves or to a being outside of them in which this compatibility is ultimately founded?

Even as mere possibles they have entity and reality, they are metaphysical beings; but as such they are no less contingent than they would be if they were actually existing beings in the physical order. In fact, they are more so because they have not the complete reality of a physical being but only the incomplete essence of a metaphysical one. They cannot, then, be the ultimate ground or reason for their own being any more than any other contingent being can be the ultimate ground for its own being. They must, then, be dependent on something outside of themselves, which is the ultimate reason for all reality, metaphysical as well as physical. This being is God, *ens perfectissimum.*

This can be stated more formally as follows. All contingent beings, including the possibles, must receive their being from another. Only God is not a contingent being and has being from Himself *(ens a se).* Therefore only God can be the ultimate ground of intrinsic possibility. If this were not so, it would mean that the omnipotence of God *(ens a se)* would be dependent on His creatures *(entia ab alio)* for the existence of His powers, which is clearly absurd.

The unity of God, as we know from natural theology, must be the unity of perfect simplicity, and hence the powers of God of which we speak are not distinct from God Himself. Nevertheless our partial concepts represent His infinity as far as we are able, since all the perfections we predicate of Him are really in His infinite essence.

One important question remains to be answered. Under what aspect of God do the possibles depend on Him, according to our way of considering the matter *(secundum nostrum modum concipiendi)?* This much-controverted problem is discussed in the sections that follow.

Is God's omnipotence the ultimate ground?

The various perfections of God, such as His omnipotence, His eternity, His simplicity, and so forth, are logically distinct from one another and from His essence. Some scholastic philosophers, among them William of Ockham (1280-1349), defended the doctrine that intrinsic possibility depended ultimately on God's omnipotence. They did not mean that such internal possibility was produced by His power, but they simply ignored the internal possibility of things altogether and said that things were intrinsically possible solely because God's power could produce them.

Such a doctrine is manifestly false because it would limit the infinite power of God. If things are possible because His power can produce them, then things that are impossible must be impossible because His power does not extend to them. But this is obviously to set limits to the divine power, and is therefore a denial of its infinity.

Further, if we admit that God's omnipotence is the ultimate ground of intrinsic possibility, we are faced with a dilemma. Either God lacks power because He cannot produce certain things, and that is why they are impossible; or He can produce beings whose essential notes are contradictory, and then there would be no impossible beings at all. In the first alternative we deny the omnipotence of God, and in the second we deny the principle of contradiction. We must admit, therefore, that the ultimate ground of intrinsic possibility is not the omnipotence of God insofar as it can be distinguished from His other perfections.

Is the will of God the ultimate ground?

According to René Descartes (1596-1650) a thing is possible because God wills it to be so, and it would be impossible if He had willed it otherwise. This doctrine of Descartes would maintain that the whole metaphysical order was necessary only on the supposition that God had willed it that way. The metaphysical order, however, is absolutely necessary independently of the will of God. Hence the intrinsic possibility of things, which is part of that metaphysical order, does not depend on the free will of God. That order is absolutely necessary because it expresses the relation of the essences of things among themselves—for instance, that twice two is four, that the whole is greater than the part, that a thing cannot be greater than itself. Such principles as those of contradiction, excluded middle, sufficient reason, causality, and all principles of intrinsic morality are part of the metaphysical order and, as such, are independent of the will of God. Descartes, on the contrary, affirmed that it was the will of God that determined that the three angles of a triangle should be equal to two right angles and that He could have willed it otherwise if He had so chosen. Such a doctrine is manifestly absurd and would destroy the foundation of all being and of all knowledge.

What we have said is not in any way opposed to the omnipotence of God. For God to be able to do what involves a contradiction in terms, to do what is unreasonable, would not be a perfection but an imperfection.

Is the intelligence of God the ultimate ground?

A quite general opinion among the older scholastics was that the intrinsic possibility of essences is formally constituted by the act in which the divine intellect, contemplating the divine essence, understands that it is infinitely imitable *ad extra;* so that, as the actuality of things is the result of the divine will, and as their extrinsic possibility is grounded in the divine omnipotence, so their intrinsic possibility is grounded in the divine intellect. The divine intellect in that case would not only give ideal being in the subjective sense to the intrinsic possibility of essences, but it would moreover make those essences formally possible, they being only virtually possible in the divine essence insofar as it is considered antecedently to this act of the divine intellect.

Others, and especially some of the more recent scholastic writers, agree that the possibles have ideal being in the divine intellect from the fact that they are objects of the divine knowledge, but they would call this ideal being subjective only, the representation: and would insist that the possibles are formally constituted in the objective order antecedently to this act of the divine intellect; that they have formal metaphysical being in the objective sense *(esse formale metaphysicum objectivum)* before the divine intellect can make them objects of thought, they, then, being the things represented. And we must not forget that they are things in the real objective metaphysical sense; otherwise we shall have to go back and start all over again from some other foundation.

It is a fundamental misconception of the nature of intelligence, whether divine or human, to maintain that it produces its own object of thought. A thing to be understood must be understandable; for the intellect to represent something, there must be a thing to represent; intellection presupposes intelligibility. In other words, if God can think of a thing as possible, it is and must be possible; but that does not mean that the intellect confers compatibility upon the possible being. Rather, intelligence can know a thing only because it is intelligible in itself *(in se ipso);* that is, because it is a being whose essence is constituted of elements that are compatible and for that reason has a positive thought content. Being of some kind is logically prior to thought because thought must conform to the thing thought of. A representation presupposes a thing in the objective order that is represented. Possible essences are not intrinsically possible because they are understood by and have ideal subjective being in the human mind; neither are they intrinsically possible because they are understood by and have ideal subjective being in the divine mind.

The essence of God, the ultimate ground of intrinsic possibility

That the essence of God is the ultimate ground of all intrinsic possibility can now be proved by exclusion or elimination. God under some aspect of His infinite being must be the ultimate ground. But it is neither His omnipotence, His will, nor His intellect; therefore it must be under some aspect which is logically prior to all these, and that can be only His essence.

Again, the divine essence is capable of being imitated, and all contingent perfection must be an imitation of it and eminently contained in it; otherwise the divine essence would not be infinite. An infinite being contains the fullness of perfection, and therefore necessarily contains all the perfections of other beings in its essence. Now, the thing which is imitated must be the ground or reason for all imitations of it. The possible, then, as a being, an essence, must be grounded in the essence of God.

The possibles, as beings in themselves *(entia in se ipsis)* are a proximate ground for intrinsic possibility. Intrinsic possibility consists in the compatibility or sociability of notes or terms. The terms are compatible because each of them is an essence of some kind—that is, opposed to nothing—and because the essences are just such as they are, since if they were otherwise, they might be incompatible and therefore nonbeings. The conclusion is that the possibles are formally constituted by the essences of things, these essences being ultimately dependent on the divine essence.

SUMMARY OF CHAPTER IV

1 One of the primary determinations of being is its division into act and potency. An act is any entity perfecting a thing in its respective order of being. This includes all powers or faculties, all operations, all accidents, essence and existence, whatever a being has or is—any perfection.

Potency is the capacity or aptitude for something. It is related to act as the incomplete to the completing, the perfectible to the perfecting, the determinable to the determining.

2 **Kinds of potency.** Objective potency is the capacity of a nonexistent being for existence. Subjective potency is the capacity of an existing being for further perfection. Subjective potency may be either receptive or operative, the former being the capacity to receive an act, and the latter being the capacity to perform one.

3 **Possibility or objective potency.** For a being to be possible in the full sense it is required and sufficient that there be a compatibility of its notes or terms and that there exist an efficient cause capable of producing it. The first constitutes its intrinsic possibility; the second constitutes its extrinsic possibility.

4 **Entity and reality of possible being.** The possibles do not exist in the physical order, yet that does not make them identical with nothing. They have the capacity for existence, whereas *nothing* has no such capacity; the possibles have an essence, a positive thought content, whereas *nothing* is at best a mere negation; the possibles differ among themselves in the metaphysical order, whereas between *nothing* and *nothing* there is no real difference. The possibles thus have real, objective, metaphysical being in themselves *(entia realia metaphysica objectiva)*.

5 Ultimate extrinsic possibility must lie outside of created things. It is placed in the omnipotence of God, insofar as our minds distinguish this from His essence.

6 **Ultimate intrinsic possibility.** The ultimate reason for the compatibility of notes of a created being must be found in God under some aspect of His infinite perfection. It cannot be found in the possible beings themselves because they are contingent beings.

God's omnipotence is not the ultimate ground, as Ockham said. If it were, then the only reason anything would be impossible would be because God could not produce it; but this would be a denial of His omnipotence.

God's will is not the ultimate ground, as was the opinion of Descartes. If this were admitted, then God could will that the impossibles become possible. Such an opinion is absurd. It would destroy the whole metaphysical order, the foundation of all being and truth.

Nor can God's intelligence be the ultimate ground of intrinsic possibility, as a number of scholastic writers have thought. According to this opinion things would be possible because God thinks them and impossible because He does not or cannot think them. This position is also absurd, for the thing known must be logically prior to the knowledge of it. The intellect presupposes its object and merely recognizes compatibility of notes; it does not confer this compatibility. The possible being has reality in the objective metaphysical order; hence it can be an object of thought for the divine mind.

The essence of God, then, must be the ultimate ground of all intrinsic possibility. It is logically prior to His omnipotence, will, and intelligence. In addition, the possible essence is an imitation of the divine essence; hence that must be its final ground and reason.

CHAPTER V

THE SUPREME PRINCIPLES OF BEING

IN this chapter we shall take time to draw some important conclusions from what has been discussed so far. The principles enunciated here are treated also in other branches of philosophy, especially in logic and epistemology. They are considered in logic as laws of thought and in epistemology as necessary foundations for truth. Here we shall consider them more generally, but especially as laws of being which are immediately derived from the concept of being.

Nature of a Principle

A principle in general is that from which something proceeds in some way. Two things are required in a principle. The first is that it must be prior to the reality which proceeds from it; the second is that it must have some connection with this reality.

It is possible to distinguish four ways in which a principle can be prior to that which proceeds from it, three of them real and one logical *(rationis)*. There is priority of *time* when the principle is in existence before the existence of that which proceeds from it; for instance, Philip existed before Alexander, and Amsterdam was prior to New Amsterdam. Priority of *nature* is had when the existence of a second thing depends on the existence of the first; for example, soul and body are prior in nature to the man they compose, the divine essence is prior in nature to the possibles, a substance is prior in nature to the accidents inhering in it. Priority of *origin* exists when there is priority neither of time nor of nature but only of procession of the one from the other. Priority of origin is found nowhere except in the Holy Trinity, in which Father, Son, and Holy Spirit are all coeternal and all equal in nature, although the Son proceeds from the Father and the Holy Spirit from the Father and the Son. One thing is said to be *logically* prior to another thing when it is prior neither in time nor in nature, but only according to our manner of thought, with some foundation in the thing; for example, the divine essence is logically prior to the divine attributes.

The connection between the principle and that which proceeds from it may be either logical or ontological. It is a logical connection when the truth of one statement depends on the truth of another; thus the premises of a syllogism are a logical principle for the conclusion, and the steps in a geometrical proof are a logical principle for the law that is formulated. It is a real or ontological connection when the being of one thing depends on the being of another; the connection that exists between cause and effect is a real or ontological one.

The principle of contradiction

The first of the principles derived from the nature of the concept of being is the principle of contradiction. It is derived from a comparison of the idea of being with the idea of nothing or nonbeing. They are evidently opposed; they mutually exclude each other with absolute necessity. If being could be nonbeing, there would be no foundation for knowledge because then everything could also be its opposite, and there could be no truth nor certitude. Our reason would thus be useless. The principle of contradiction may be stated as follows: It is impossible for a thing to be and not be at the same time and under the same aspect *(sub eodem respectu)*. This could also be expressed as under the same circumstances, under the same conditions, or in the same respect. Rain could fall and not fall at the same time; it usually does, but not if we refer to exactly the same place. Either it rains or it does not rain at this time in this spot. Christ is either God or not God. To commit murder, to perjure oneself when testifying in court, or to take what belongs to another without his knowledge and consent and without any justifying cause is either morally wrong or morally justifiable. If one is true, the other is false, for they are contradictories; they affirm and deny the same thing under the same aspect.

The principle of contradiction applies universally to all being, the finite and the infinite, the material and the spiritual. It is the foundation of all being and of all knowledge, self-evident and not requiring proof. In fact, this principle is incapable of proof precisely because it is immediately evident to the mind. It is the foundation of our rejection of the position of the skeptics. If the principle of contradiction were not admitted, it would be impossible to advance one step on the road to knowledge.

The principle of excluded middle

The principle of the excluded middle is usually expressed as follows: Between being and nonbeing there is no middle or third thing possible. This also follows from the very nature of being and is an evident corollary of the principle of contradiction. The understanding of the concepts of being and nonbeing is sufficient to make it immediately evident. If it is impossible for a thing to be and not be under the same aspect, then such a thing must either be or not be. The principle of excluded middle is, in fact, just another way of expressing the principle of contradiction. If the latter is evident, the former must be evident also. In expressing a contradiction we see at once that there is no middle ground. Christ is either God or not God, a certain religion is either true or not true, a certain distinction is either real or not real. We must be careful, however, that we have a real contradiction. Statements may be not contradictories but only contraries, and therefore may admit a middle position. Christ is either God or man; a religion is either true or not good in any manner; a distinction is either real or without any foundation in reality. If the statement expresses a real contradiction, then it admits of no middle ground; if it is true, its contradictory is necessarily false.

The principle of sufficient reason

The principle of sufficient reason is stated thus: Everything must have a sufficient reason for its being or existence. This is again a corollary of the nature of being as opposed to nonbeing. If there were no sufficient reason for the reality of a being, it would mean that the being in question had received the reality which it has from nonbeing, nothing, the absence of reality. Now, this is obviously impossible. *Nothing* has no reality in itself and therefore could not possibly give reality to another. A being without a sufficient reason is thus a contradiction in terms; it would both be and not be under the same aspect. By supposition it would be a being, a reality. But as a being without a sufficient reason, it would be a nonbeing or nothing because it could have only that reality which nothing could give, which is precisely none at all. A being without a sufficient reason would amount to a being which is a nonbeing, since it would have reality neither from itself nor from another being. There can, then, be no being or reality without a sufficient reason for its being or reality.

The principle of causality

This principle will be treated at greater length in a later chapter, but it is mentioned here because it is an obvious application of the principle of sufficient reason.

The principle of causality is the principle of sufficient reason applied to beings which come into existence. It is usually stated in these terms: Whatever passes from a state of nonexistence into a state of existence must have an efficient cause for its existence. This principle follows immediately from the principle of sufficient reason because without an efficient cause there would be no sufficient reason for the existence of the new reality.

Like the other principles of being, the principle of causality can readily be reduced to the principle of contradiction. The new reality could have received existence either from nothing, or from itself, or from another being. To say that it received existence from *nothing* is absurd. If it received existence from *itself,* it would have had to be in act before it existed; that is, it would have to exist before it existed, which is absurd and a violation of the principle of contradiction. Therefore it must have received existence from another being which produced it. But this is its efficient cause.

The principle of identity

Some modern philosophers have added to the foregoing what they call the principle of identity, which they formulate in this fashion: Being is being, and nonbeing is nonbeing. We shall discuss later the nature of identity and distinction. Here it will be sufficient to remark that the so-called principle of identity, insofar as it is not merely tautological, expresses the same idea which is contained implicitly in the principle of contradiction. When we say that whatever is, is, we really mean that it must necessarily be what it is and cannot be its contradictory; to say this is merely expressing the principle of contradiction in another way. The principle of identity, then, is already contained in the principle of contradiction as an implicit affirmative statement of what the principle of contradiction states in a negative manner. We thus cannot agree with those who would make the principle of identity the primary and most fundamental principle. According to almost unanimous opinion that distinction belongs to the principle of contradiction.

The principle of contradiction is the primary and most fundamental principle of being and of thought precisely because it is based, as we have said, on the nature of the idea of being as distinguished from *nothing*. The idea of being is the first idea in the logical order as being itself is first in the ontological order; therefore the principle which immediately depends on it is the most basic principle in those orders. The principle of contradiction is implicitly contained in every judgment; and unless it has been previously accepted, it would be impossible to make a judgment. The world of being and of thought stands or falls with the principle of contradiction.

From what has been said it is clear that these principles are primarily principles of reality, but they also have a logical character: they are laws of thought as well as of being. This is necessarily true, for ideas are mental representations of things and must conform to reality. The truth of things must regulate the truth of thought. The mind must be determined by extramental reality; otherwise we would be living in a dream world. The laws of being, therefore, must also be laws of thought. These laws of being are expressed as laws of thought in logic. The principle of contradiction is stated thus: Something cannot be both true and false at the same time and under the same aspect; contradictories cannot both be true. The principle of excluded middle is formulated thus: Contradictory judgments must be either true or false; if one is true, the other must be false. The principle of sufficient reason is expressed in logical terms as follows: There must be a sufficient reason why a judgment is true or false.

The doctrine of Hegel

The great adversary in modern times of practically all the previous doctrine is Georg Hegel (1770-1831), German exponent of what is usually called evolutionary idealistic pantheism. A great number of others follow him in this system of philosophy, all of them, just as he did, starting with Kantian idealism as a foundation. Some of the more prominent names are Fichte, Schelling, Schopenhaüer, Hartmann, Nietzsche, Green, and Royce. Hegel's teaching is filled with contradictions, but it nevertheless deserves our attention for two reasons: first because it has influenced so many philosophers in the United States as well as in other countries; and second because its many inconsistencies serve to accentuate the reasonableness and coherence of scholastic thought.

The following statements from Hegel's writings on logic are illustrative of his doctrine:

> The distinction between Being and Nought is, in the first place, only implicit, and not yet actually made: they only *ought* to be distinguished. A distinction of course implies

> two things, and that one of them possesses an attribute which is not found in the other. Being however is an absolute absence of attributes, and so is Nought. Hence the distinction between the two is only meant to be; it is a quite nominal distinction, which is at the same time no distinction. In all other cases of difference there is some common point which comprehends both things. Suppose *e.g.* we speak of two different species: the genus forms a common ground for both. But in the case of mere Being and Nothing, distinction is without a bottom to stand upon: hence there can be no distinction, both determinations being the same bottomlessness. . . . Being is not a particular or definite thought, and hence, being quite indeterminate, is a thought not to be distinguished from nothing. . . . Nothing, if it be thus immediate and equal to itself, is also conversely the same as Being is. . . . In Being then we have Nothing, and in Nothing Being. . . . In Becoming the Being which is one with Nothing, and the Nothing which is one with Being, are only vanishing factors: they are and they are not.[1]

According to Hegel, *being* is identical with *nothing* because it is indeterminate and refers, therefore, to no determinate being. But this is an obvious absurdity. The fact that the idea of being in general *(ens ut sic)* is indeterminate does not disprove the fact that it has a positive content, that it has at least a relation to existence, that it could exist. It could not, of course, exist as it is in the mind, as general and indeterminate *(quoad modum quo);* but that which it expresses *(quoad id quod)* exists or could exist. If given existence, it must of course be a specific and determined existence. The concept of being

[1] *Logic of Hegel,* translated by William Wallace, pp. 162-63, 167, 169. London: Oxford University Press, 1931.

nevertheless expresses a reality just as the direct universal does.

Again, if the ideas of *being* and absolute *nothing* are identical, then whatever is excluded from the idea of absolute nothing would also be excluded from the idea of indeterminate being. But this has been shown to be false. All being of whatever kind is excluded from absolute nothing; only determinate being is excluded from the idea of being in general. The two ideas are objectively different, one representing being and the other nonbeing. Both indeed exclude determinate being, and in this they are alike; but the idea of being has a positive thought content, a possible essence, which the idea of nothing entirely lacks. The fact that they are alike in one feature does not make them identical. Hegel's contention, then, is a contradiction in terms. It is on this contradiction, which is a denial of both fact and reason, that he bases his system of idealistic monism.

However repugnant to reason it may appear, it is Hegel's further contention that out of this idea of being, which according to him is equivalent to nothing, and by means of the principles explained in this chapter, there is a gradual unfolding and development of all determinate being. He explains it as a logical evolution of the idea of being in such wise that all particular truths and all determinate beings derive their origin from this logical evolution. In this way the supreme principles of being would constitute productive principles or causes in much the same way as if the football field, the officials, and two fully equipped football teams should grow out of the rules of football as found in the rule book. These ideas, then, would be the efficient causes of all reality. This is the old confusion of the infinite being *(ens perfectissimum)* with the idea of being in general *(ens abstractissimum)*. Hegel confuses the physical reality which contains within itself the fullness of being with the idea of being, the emptiest and most abstract of all ideas, a mental abstraction which indeed extends to all being, including the infinite, but which as a mere idea has no physical entity of any kind, and therefore could not possibly be the cause of anything, and certainly not of all reality.

The actual fact is that these principles are not causes but regulative norms or laws to which all particular beings and truths, all thought and reality, must conform. The origin or cause of particular beings cannot be found in these principles. They must have their source of being entirely outside these principles. These principles are not the cause of the universe; but if and when the universe exists, it must be governed by these principles or laws. It cannot exist and not exist at the same time and under the same aspect; it either exists or it does not exist; and it must have a sufficient reason for its existence outside of itself because it is not a self-existent being. The reality of the universe is not due to these principles, but that reality is regulated by these laws. The idea of being in general, if properly understood, may lead the mind to the idea of the infinite; but it is the *physical reality* of the infinite and not its *idea* which is the cause of the universe.

SUMMARY OF CHAPTER V

1 **Nature of a principle.** A principle is that from which something proceeds in some way. A principle must be prior to

that which proceeds from it. There is priority of time, of nature, of origin, and of reason *(rationis)*. The supreme principles of being are those which are immediately derived from the concept of being.

2 **Principle of contradiction.** A thing cannot be and not be something at the same time and under the same aspect. The principle of contradiction is the primary and most fundamental principle of all thought and of all being.

3 **Principle of excluded middle.** A thing either is or is not. Between being and nonbeing there is no middle or third thing possible.

4 **Principle of sufficient reason.** Everything must have a sufficient reason for its being or existence.

5 **Principle of causality.** Whatever passes from a state of nonexistence to a state of existence must have an efficient cause; otherwise it would violate the principles of sufficient reason and contradiction.

6 These principles are also logical principles because our thoughts, if they are to be true, must be regulated by reality.

7 Georg Hegel identified being with *nothing* because, as he said, they both exclude determinate being. He failed to realize that being is not nonbeing, that it has a positive thought content or essence which *nothing* lacks.

The supreme principles of being are not the producing causes of reality, as Hegel thought, but they are laws according to which reality must be regulated if it exists.

CHAPTER VI

THE PRINCIPLE OF CHANGE

THE nature of change was one of the earliest problems discussed by philosophers. As far back as the sixth century B.C. the Eleatics answered the problem by embracing pantheism, holding that there is only one reality and that it is absolutely unchangeable. Thus they denied that there was any such thing as change in nature and held that what appeared to be change was an illusion. On the other hand, at about the same time Heraclitus was teaching that there was only becoming and no permanent reality at all. According to him everything was in a continuous state of change, and this was the only reality. There was no being; there was only becoming.

It was in order to explain the reality of being and becoming, of a permanent reality which was subject to change, that Aristotle formulated his doctrine of potency and act. According to that analysis all finite beings are composites of potency and act. From mere objective potency they can come into existence. When they have existence they are still perfectible to a greater or less degree. Hence they are continually passing from potency to act; there is a constant becoming and continual change.

In order to bring out more strongly the force of the Aristotelian answer to the problem of change, it will be helpful to explain the difficulty and the various answers to it in greater detail. We observe that everything about us is subject to change, is constantly in motion. This is true of the inanimate world, as well as of the animate world in which there is the continual process of birth, growth, and death. Our senses testify to the fact of local motion as well as to greater and more fundamental mutations in the world around us. Is this testimony correct and, if so, what is motion or change? How does a thing become what it was not before? Parmenides answered these questions by denying the fact of motion or change and asserting that it was only so in appearance, an illusion of the senses. Motion and change are impossible, he said in effect. In change there is supposedly something new which is produced by the change. But such production is absurd. Before the change that thing which is produced or becomes either was or was not. If it existed previously, it was not produced. If it did not exist previously, it was nonbeing; that is, nothing. If it was nothing, obviously nothing could come of it; that is, something cannot be produced from nothing. Thus Parmenides and the Eleatic school answered the problem. Heraclitus proposed the opposite opinion. According to him everything was change or becoming, and that was the only reality. Being was not real; there was only a constant flux.

The solutions of both Parmenides and Heraclitus lead to the same conclusions—skepticism and pantheism. The doctrine of Parmenides leads to skepticism because it denies the validity of intellectual knowledge. Pantheism in the thought of Parmenides takes the form of an assertion of the existence of only one being, the changeless or infinite; the teaching of Heraclitus likewise results in pantheism, but the one existing reality is now dynamic, always in flux. It is interesting to recall that both these types of pantheism have continued to find adherents throughout the ages and that they are still with us in the doctrines of Hegel and Spencer.

How can this Scylla and Charybdis, both of which are death, be avoided? Plato attempted a solution with his doctrine of the Ideas, which are supposed to mediate between determinate and indeterminate reality. As we shall see in greater detail later, there was some merit in this solution. Although Plato exaggerated the reality of the idea, he insisted nonetheless that it did have some reality, and he thus prepared the way for the doctrine of Aristotle. The credit for arriving at the true answer belongs to Aristotle, who developed the doctrine of potency and act. To the difficulty of Parmenides that that which becomes was either being or nonbeing Aristotle replied with a distinction: it was either *being in act* or *being in potency,* both of them being real in some sense; it was not nonbeing. This assertion of the reality of being in potency is the key to the whole philosophical riddle. Being in act is what it is, and therefore cannot "become" what it already is. Being in potency, however, can by a process of change become being in act and vice versa. The marble can become a statue because it is in potency to becoming such; and unless that potency were something real in the marble, the statue could never exist. Aristotle, therefore, explained the process of change in the passage from potency to act, from the capacity for perfection to the realization of the perfection.

Change in the strict sense is the transition from one positive state of being to another. Three conditions are required for a strict change: (1) a positive starting point *(terminus a quo)*. In a strict change there must be an actual being with a potency for some new state or act; (2) a positive goal or terminus *(terminus ad quem)*. It is required that the final state of the being also be actual, with a newly acquired state or act; (3) a real transition in the sense that there is a physical change from one state to the other; that is, there must be a passage from potency to act in a physical being.

Thus creation is not a change in the strict sense, nor would annihilation be considered a strict change. For if the starting point is a state of nonexistence, we would have the production of a thing from no presupposed starting point or *terminus a quo*. In the case of annihilation the *terminus ad quem* would be a state of nonexistence. A third kind of change in the wide sense of the word is called extrinsic change. In this type of change there is no real transition in the being which is said to change, but rather in another being which is in some way related to it. For instance, when one person has his automobile painted to resemble that of another, the second vehicle is said to change extrinsically or externally because it is now similar to the first where before it had been dissimilar. So too if one person in a family becomes a princess, the other members are said to change extrinsically although only one member has really changed. All of these would be changes in a wide sense, but not in the strict sense.

Kinds of strict change

There are several kinds of change in the strict sense:

Generation and corruption. When a being changes from one kind of substantial entity into another kind of substantial entity, the change of the first substance is called corruption and the change of the second substance is called generation. They are but two aspects of the same thing, a substantial change. The new substance is generated through the corruption of the old. Such a change takes place in the life and death of animals and plants. The chemical elements are changed into organic matter, part of the living tissue of the organism; and when the organism dies, they again change from living matter into inorganic chemical elements.

Augmentation and diminution. These are transitions from one quantitative state of being to another. If the quantity increases, the change is called augmentation; if the quantity decreases, it is called diminution. Such a change could happen to any material being. An acorn grows into an oak; a mustard seed develops into a tree; one loses weight through exercise.

Alteration. The transition of a being from one qualitative state to another is called alteration. The oak tree may become more or less healthy, its leaves change color and fall off in autumn, the muscles become firm by exercise.

Local motion. The transition of a thing from one place to another is called local motion. The boy runs, the ball rolls, the engine moves.

These last three kinds of change are accidental and successive rather than substantial. An interval of time, be it ever so small, is required for their occurrence. Aristotle defined successive change as the act of a being in potency while it is still in potency, the process of the realization of a potentiality insofar as it is still a potency. An example will make the definition clearer. Suppose some boys are running a hundred-yard dash. When they start they are in complete potentiality, but as they progress that potentiality is being more and more realized—it becomes a partial act and partial potency; when they cross the goal they are in act, and the potency for that particular race has been completely realized—they have accomplished what they set out to do. They are always in potency toward the complete act until they have crossed the finish line; the change is the act of a being in potency while still in potency. It is the actuality of a partly realized potency while still only partly realized. This definition of Aristotle is not restricted to local motion. It applies also to any successive change or transition from potency to act.

The principle of change

The principle of change was formulated by Aristotle as follows: Whatever changes is changed by another—*Quidquid movetur ab alio movetur.* Change as it is used here means any transition from potency to act and therefore includes becoming as well as strict change. It makes no difference whether the transition is from nonexistence to existence or from one positive state of being to another positive state of being; the principle applies equally in either case. In the first case it would involve the production of the whole entity without any previous physical being of its own or any subject matter of a physical nature *(ex nihilo sui et subjecti)*. There must of course be objective potentiality or possibility, which, as we have seen, is a being but not a physical one. In the second case it involves the transition of an existing thing to a different kind of being; this sort of change supposes an underlying subject (physically existing) in which the change takes place.

For the moment we shall restrict the principle of change to the receptive potencies. With this restriction the principle may be stated as follows: *Nothing ever passes from receptive potency to act except under the influence of another being which is already in act.* As far as mechanical motion is concerned, no one would dispute this. Newton's laws of motion, which are considered to be the foundation of physical science, say the same thing in a slightly different way: Every body tends to persevere in its state of rest or of uniform motion unless it is acted on by an outside force.

The philosophical proof is nothing more than the application of the principle of sufficient reason and ultimately of the principle of contradiction to the fact of change. In every change a new perfection or reality is acquired by the being which is changed. Now, there are only three possibilities of accounting for this new reality: it could come from the potential being itself, or from nothing, or from some actual being. The potential being cannot give the new reality to itself because nothing can give what it does not have. There would be no sufficient reason for the new act or perfection. And one cannot say that the being had this act before, because then the principle of contradiction would be violated—it would be in act and potency under the same aspect. Neither can *nothing* be a sufficient reason for the new act for the same reasons given above. The potential being can receive the new perfection only from some actual being which is able to communicate its actuality to the potential being.

The nature of operative potency

If we restrict the principle of change to receptive potencies, all scholastics are in agreement on the universality of its application. But there are also operative potencies, such as man's faculties or powers of intellect and will, for example. These have the appearance at least of performing their operations without the necessity of being activated by other agents. They have been said to be capable of immanent activity; that is, of actions which proceed from the living being itself and perfect it in some way.

Everyone understands that organisms are influenced by outside agencies. The senses of animals require the presence of stimuli before they can act, the intellect of man requires the presentation of an object, and the will requires the previous knowledge of the good; but these are not the efficient causes of the act. They may be occasions, conditions, or at most final causes, but they do not produce the act.

Neither does anyone deny the causality of the first cause in all creatural actions. The concurrence of the infinite in such actions is beyond dispute. The question is whether it is *concurrence* or *premotion.*

Scholastic philosophers who belong to the Thomistic school claim that the principle of change applies with equal force and rigor to both receptive and operative potencies; they say that nothing ever passes from potency to act except under the influence of another being which is already in act, and that this applies also to operative potencies. According to this view an antecedent physical influence, a physical premotion *(praemotio physica),* is required so that the faculty of a creature can pass from potentiality to actuality. This influence is supplied by God to all creatural activity, and it is only by virtue of it that the faculty is fully capable of operation.

Such a position seems at least to call into question some very fundamental doctrine. Does it not mean that the receptive potencies and the operative potencies are both on the same plane? What remains of the distinction between them? And, finally, if the creature cannot act of itself but must be moved to action by the Creator, how does this differ from the doctrine of occasionalism, which denies the self-activity of creatures and declares that creatures merely provide occasions or conditions for the activity of the infinite? On account of such difficulties many scholastic philosophers find themselves unable to accept the Thomistic view.

The Thomists defend their position by saying that the principle of sufficient reason absolutely demands the inclusion of the operative potencies in the scope of the principle of change. According to them there is no essential difference between an operative potency and a receptive potency when it is a question of acquiring a new act or perfection. The intellect and will are certainly perfected by their operations, which are acts or perfections. Since the faculty did not possess the act before, it could not give it to itself; only some other agency, then, can be a sufficient reason for this new perfection. The faculty itself cannot be the sufficient reason, for it cannot reduce itself from potentiality to actuality, and hence the principle of change applies equally to both kinds of potency. It is therefore necessary that God supply a physical premotion in order that the operative potency may become active.

Those who oppose the Thomistic view fail to see the need or usefulness of a physical premotion. They argue that such an influence merely places the faculty in immediate preparation for its act; it does not give the actual operation itself, but makes the faculty capable of operating. If this is true, then the faculty must still make the passage from potency to act, which would be contrary to the principle of change as it is interpreted by the Thomists. Why should it not be possible for the Creator to endow the creature with an adequate faculty capable of acting without a previous physical premotion, which in any event seems to be incapable of performing the function ascribed to it? If the Thomists embrace the other horn of the dilemma and assert that it is precisely the physical premotion which reduces the faculty from potency to act, then the faculty is no longer an operative faculty, but merely a receptive faculty, and so has no activity of its own. But this is a denial of the activity of creatures and amounts to the doctrine of occasionalism.

Another argument is also advanced by those who do not accept the Thomist doctrine on this point. If the operative faculty needs an outside agency (physical premotion) to reduce it to act, then the same necessity applies to this entity—it is also a creatural being and needs another being to reduce it to act. In order, then, to avoid an infinite series, it would be necessary to admit that God is the direct agent of all creatural activity, which would likewise amount to the doctrine of the occasionalists.

On the other hand, the opponents of Thomism have the difficulty of explaining the presence of the new perfection added to the faculty by its act without denying the principle of sufficient reason. To answer this difficulty they make a distinction between the virtual act and the formal act. The change which takes place when a faculty passes from potency to act is not a change in the perfection itself but in its manner of being; the change is from virtual act to formal act. Certainly the perfection of the new act is not contained formally in the faculty; but if it were not contained at least virtually in the faculty, then the faculty would not be an operative potency but merely a receptive potency. There would be no such thing as an operative potency, and therefore no true creatural activity. Thus the distinction that we here make between virtual act and formal act seems to provide the only possible solution to the problem. It is absolutely necessary to admit the presence of the act or perfection in the faculty as potency; the change which takes place is the change of the virtual act to the formal act.

We have already discussed the doctrine of Hegel with regard to *being* and *nothing*. His explanation of becoming and change is equally interesting and instructive. He writes in the *Logic:* "Being is not a particular or definite thought, and hence, being quite indeterminate, is a thought not to be distinguished from Nothing."[1] But being does not remain in the indeterminate state—it *becomes*. "Becoming is the first concrete thought, and therefore the first notion: whereas Being and Nought are empty abstractions."[2]

According to Hegel this "becoming" then gives rise to determinate being by a process of logical evolution which unfolds into matter and spirit and eventually develops into the absolute, which is Hegelian for God.

> Even our ordinary conception of Becoming implies that somewhat [something] comes out of it, and that Becoming therefore has a result. . . . Becoming always contains Being and Nothing in such a way, that these two are always changing into each other, and reciprocally cancelling each other. Thus Becoming stands before us in utter restlessness . . . for since Being and Nothing vanish in Becoming (and that is the very notion of Becoming), the latter must vanish. . . . The result of this process however is not an empty Nothing, but Being identical with the negation,—what we call Being Determinate (being then and there): the primary import of which evidently is that it *has become*.[3]

This language is very remote indeed from the speech of ordinary men, but we must expect this in pantheists like Hegel. Let us paraphrase the thought in words to which

[1] *Logic of Hegel,* p. 163.
[2] *Ibid.,* p. 167.
[3] *Ibid.,* p. 170.

we may be more accustomed. Hegel begins with the idea of being, and since he takes it for granted that both the idea and the reality of being are one and the same thing (a confusion of the ideal with the real, or, in more technical language, of the metaphysical with the physical), he holds that it actually develops itself from indeterminateness to determinate being by means of a logical process of internal evolution. At first being is so indeterminate that it is equivalent to nothing, but through this process of logical evolution (becoming) it gradually gives rise to every kind of determinate being. The process is one of the self-actualization of the idea of being.

"Being" as described by Hegel must be either logical or ontological (metaphysical). As a logical being it is abstract, indeterminate, empty of content, "equivalent to Nothing." If it is such, it is a contradiction that anything should arise out of it, that determinate being could ever be deduced from it. As a metaphysical or ontological being it must be devoid of all actuality and therefore purely potential. It is not the infinite, containing within itself all actuality in some way—it is in Hegel's own words "empty Nothing." But this "Nothing" or at best purely potential being is supposed to develop into all real being. This is such an obvious absurdity that it requires no formal refutation.

SUMMARY OF CHAPTER VI

1 **The concept of change.** Change in a broad sense is any transition from potency to act. In a strict sense change is the transition from potency to act in a material being in

successive stages. Aristotle defined strict change in classic terms as the act of a being in potency while still in potency. It is the actuality of a potential being insofar as it is still potential. For strict change three conditions are required: a positive starting point, a positive terminus, and a real transition from the one to the other. Creation, annihilation, and extrinsic change are changes only in a broad sense.

2 **Kinds of strict change.** Generation and corruption are transitions of a being from one kind of substantial entity to another. Augmentation and diminution are quantitative changes; alteration is a qualitative change. Local motion is the transition from one place to another.

3 The principle of change may be stated as follows: Whatever is changed is changed by another. No being passes from receptive potency to act except under the influence of another being already in act. This is admitted by physical science at least with regard to mechanical motion. It is proved by reason in this manner: Every act acquired is a new perfection or reality, and there must be a sufficient reason for it. But this sufficient reason is not in the potential being, because if it possessed the act before the change, it would not be in potency for that act. It can receive it, therefore, only from another being already in act.

4 Thomistic scholastics apply the principle of change to the operative potencies also and postulate a physical premotion to assist the creatural faculty in its passage from potency to act. Such an entity would be supplied by God. Other scholastics fail to see the force of this reasoning, which seems to deny immanent activity in living things, to reduce all potency to receptive potency, and to call in question all creatural activity, which is the position of the occasionalists. The opponents of the Thomists explain the presence of the new perfection by saying that it is contained virtually in

the faculty, and that the change is from a virtual act to a formal act.

5 Hegel's doctrine of change is contradictory and absurd. He attempts to deduce all being from the idea of being in general by a logical process of evolution. Since his being in general is equivalent to *nothing* and is at best entirely potential, its self-actualization into all determinate being is contrary to the principle of change as well as the principle of contradiction.

CHAPTER VII

ESSENCE AND EXISTENCE

WE have been using the terms *essence* and *existence* constantly in the preceding pages. Let us now examine these concepts more thoroughly in order to understand better what they and other related ideas really express. A possible being is one that has an essence, which has a capacity for existence without yet having come into existence. Whatever is possible is an essence, and an essence must always be a possible being because it has compatibility of notes. Only an essence is possible. Hence an essence and a possible are one and the same thing, and they both have real being of the metaphysical kind. An actual being is one that has existence, the capacity of the possible being having been realized. Existence, then, is an act, a determination, a perfection, a new state of being for a possible or an essence. A possible being is in objective potency for an existential act; an actual being is in possession of the existential act. The one has actual, physical being; the other has possible, metaphysical being: both have reality, but of different kinds.

After an explanation of essence and existence we will consider the nature of the distinction between them. Many authors in recent years have omitted a discussion of this famous controversy. We gave careful consideration to such a procedure, but finally decided that the discussion was sufficiently important and fruitful to be included.

Definition of essence

The essence of a thing cannot be perceived by the senses. Through the senses we can only learn some of the being's individuating notes, as they are called; from these accidental properties we can, by the use of the intellect, reason to or infer the essence. We must analyze what we know of a being until we arrive at those elements which are absolutely required and suffice to make it what it is and distinguish it from other things. These are its essential notes, its essence. Essence, then, is defined as that by which a thing is what it is *(id quo res est id quod est).*

We have seen before that the essence of man is to be a rational animal. *Animal* is his genus and *rational* is his specific difference. This definition by proximate genus and specific difference is called an essential definition because it states the essence. The essence of a thing is also sometimes called the *nature* because all other things are considered to flow from or be born out of the essence; thus essence is called nature when it is considered as the ultimate principle of operation in a being. The essence of a thing is often called *quiddity,* which is a transliteration of the Latin term *quidditas,* formed from the interrogative *quid* (what). The reason is that the essence is the answer to the question, "What is it—*Quid est res?*" Sometimes the words *essence* and *substance* are used as synonyms. Substance is of course the primary reality in a being, and it is that which constitutes the essence. Accidents, however, also have an essence, that which makes them what they are, and therefore this usage might be ambiguous.

Kinds of essence

Essence is designated by giving the parts of which a being is composed. We may speak of two kinds of essence, physical and metaphysical. If we give the physical parts of a being as they exist concretely in nature, we have the physical essence; for instance, man is composed of body and soul, two incomplete physical parts. If we give the metaphysical parts, the genus and species, we have the metaphysical essence; for example, man is a rational animal. The metaphysical essence of a being is the same as the essential definition of the being. It is composed of the various grades of metaphysical being that are verified in the particular being in question. These metaphysical grades of being are objectively different concepts, each of which constitutes a possible being, as does also the composite essence. They do not mutually include each other, but can be verified separately in other beings. In any particular existing being the metaphysical parts are of course inseparable from the being. They are called metaphysical parts because they have real metaphysical being. They are not logical parts as, for instance, are being and *per se* in the concept of substance. This point will be explained more fully in Chapter 8.

Properties of metaphysical essences

Essences are spoken of as having the properties of immutability, indivisibility, necessity, and eternity.

Essences are immutable in the sense that they are what they are and cannot be otherwise. No constituent note can be taken away from or added to an essence without destroying that particular essence. The essence of man is to be a rational animal. If either note were removed, it would cease to be that essence; it would not be man but some other being.

The property of being indivisible is the same in reality as that of being immutable. If an essence could be divided, it would be changed, and would not remain the same essence.

The same is true of necessity. The necessity that belongs to an essence is of course not absolute necessity, since this can belong only to the infinite, an actually existing physical being. It is an hypothetical necessity, by which we mean that an essence must be composed of the essential elements that are proper to it and of no other. An essence is necessarily what it is and cannot be otherwise, precisely because it is immutable.

The eternity of essences also follows from their immutability. This simply means that essences are independent of time, that they must always have been and must always be what they are now; otherwise they would not be the same essences. Here again it is necessary to note that essences have no positive eternity in the same sense that God has it, as actually existing infinite beings, but only a negative or potential eternity in the sense that they are indifferent to existence in any particular portion of time.

It should be evident that these properties belong also to possible beings. Possible beings are equally immutable and eternal precisely because they are metaphysical essences. If a possible being were to be changed essentially, it might no longer be possible; its notes might then not be compatible.

The meaning of existence

An essence is a being that can exist. While it remains in the metaphysical order without existence it has only possible being. If by the power of an adequate producing cause it ceases to be a mere possibility and comes into the order of actual physical things, it is said to exist. Your state of being is that of existence; the state of being of your grandson is that of essence or possibility. Existence, therefore, can be described as that state of a being in virtue of which it is present as an actuality in the physical order, and not merely as a possibility in the metaphysical order.

The distinction between essence and existence

It is clear that the essence of the infinite must include existence; otherwise it would not be the infinite being. In God essence and existence are absolutely identical. If we make any distinction, it must be a mental or logical one.

Without doubt the two concepts are different, and there is a foundation even in God for distinguishing them.

The problem here concerns these two ideas in connection with finite being. The question is whether the distinction between essence and existence in an actually existing finite being is a real distinction or merely a mental or logical one. In order to understand the difficulty it will be necessary to anticipate some of the material from a later chapter where the whole problem of distinctions is treated more fully.

A real distinction exists when objects are different independently of the mind. The mind merely recognizes the distinction which already exists in objective reality. There is a real distinction between James and John, between soul and body in man.

A mental or logical distinction exists when the distinction depends at least partially on the mind. Such a distinction is often called virtual, but we prefer not to use that term although we mention it here.[1] There are two kinds of logical distinction with a foundation in reality, and the difference between them is important and crucial. According to most scholastics one kind of logical distinction has a perfect foundation in reality and the other has only an imperfect foundation in reality.

Both parties to the dispute concerning the distinction between essence and existence agree that there is a real

[1] The reason we do not wish to speak of a logical distinction as a virtual distinction is that opponents of Thomism who use this terminology frequently fail to distinguish between the two types of logical or virtual distinction. It may usually be taken for granted that when these authors speak of a virtual distinction they are referring to a logical distinction with only an imperfect foundation in reality.

distinction between the essence in the possible order and the same essence in the actual, physical order; they disagree regarding the nature of the distinction between the essence and the existence of an actually existing finite being. The question may be stated as follows: Are essence and existence in this particular man two distinct realities or only one reality with a foundation in the object for a mental distinction? Thomists say that the distinction is real. Others follow Suarez in saying that it is only logical.

The problem is admittedly a difficult one and perhaps does not have the great practical importance with which it has sometimes been regarded. Nevertheless it is an interesting and important historical controversy and one of which the student should be aware.

Cardinal Mercier is an exponent of the case for the real distinction. Here are his two basic arguments:

> [1.] Essence—what a thing is—is the sum of the notes expressed in the definition of a thing. Existence is existence, we cannot translate it by any other equivalent idea. Now, on the one hand, never does a definition of any object, however perfect, comprise in it the existence of the object defined. Represent anything you like in nature, not only with the notes characteristic of its species but also with its individual features; attribute to it all the reality that is requisite to give an adequate answer to the question, "What is it?" and the thing will still be destitute of existence, it will still be something capable of existing, not something actually so. On the other hand, the existence of any actual thing, though it also extends over the whole object, is one and indivisible, it is existence and only existence. . . . Hence essence does not include existence, nor existence essence; between the two

there is an adequate diversity, corresponding as they do, according to the remark of St. Thomas, to two different questions—existence to the question, *"An est?"* [Does it exist?] and essence to the question, *"Quid est?"* [What is it?]. In fine, therefore, the being which is at once the object of two adequately distinct concepts cannot be simple but must be a compound being; or, in other words, essence and existence are two component elements of an existing being.

[2.] Beings that fall under our experience are obviously finite; moreover, they are many. But a being whose essence is identical with its existence is necessarily infinite and unique. Therefore the essences of things to which our experience extends are really distinct from their existence.[2]

Cardinal Mercier also gives a third argument which he calls an "indirect" proof and which is drawn from the fact that scholastic philosophy recognizes the existence of composite beings that are also real units. Such is a corporeal being made up of matter and form. Now if every reality had its existence, and accordingly the matter and form each had its own existence, they could not make up a body substantially one. Therefore their unity must be accounted for by one act of existence, which is not the existence of each part but of the whole. It follows therefore, concludes the cardinal, that the existence of the body must be distinct from the essence which is the matter and form.[3]

The first argument of Cardinal Mercier shows very clearly a distinction of concept between essence and exist-

[2] D. Cardinal Mercier, *Manual of Modern Scholastic Philosophy,* translated by T. L. Parker and S. A. Parker, second edition, Vol. 1, pp. 435-36. London: Kegan Paul, Trench, Trubner and Company; St. Louis: B. Herder Book Company, 1921.

[3] *Ibid.,* pp. 438-39.

ence and also the real distinction of possible essence from real existence. But it does not prove that the actually existing essence is really distinct from its own existence. No one denies, for instance, that man is a compound being. He is compounded of potency and act, of matter and form, of body and soul, of animal and rational. Where is the necessity of having him compounded in still another way?

As to the second argument, the real identity of essence and existence in finite things would not make them infinite. The essence of the finite being was and is contingent; if its existence is identified with its essence, it must also be contingent.

With regard to the third argument, the scholastic theory of matter and form does not attribute existence to incomplete substances such as matter and form. Everyone agrees that there is but one existence in the composite being, the existence of the whole, not the component parts.

The arguments by which the Suarezians defend their position are proposed as follows:

1. The actual essence is not really distinct from its existence if it already exists in its own physical being. But the actual essence does already exist in its own physical being; therefore the actual essence is not really distinct from its own existence.

With regard to the major, Thomists generally agree that being and unity are not really distinct from the man who is a being and one. If therefore the actual essence already exists in its own physical reality, existence as such does not add anything physically different from it but is the same as the actual essence.

Proof of the minor: The actual essence, considered as physically distinct, which it is in the opinion of the Thomists, in itself is not nothing nor anything merely possible but a positive and actual something; but to be a positive and actual something opposed to nothing and to the merely possible is to exist.

2. That physical reality which is assumed by the Thomists to be a really distinct existence must be itself something, and indeed a contingent created being. But in such a being the reason given by them for holding the real distinction is its very contingency; therefore in that physical reality which they call existence, there must also be a real distinction between its essence and existence, and so on indefinitely.

Against the first argument the Thomists seem to maintain that when a being comes into existence its objective potency must be first changed to a subjective potency before it can receive existence. But according to the Suarezians this would be equivalent to saying that a being must be given the act of existence twice, which would evidently be a contradiction.

Thomists answer the second argument by saying that it is based on a misunderstanding. St. Thomas did not hold that existence is a being in the strict sense but rather an *ens quo,* a being by which the essence exists, and without which it could not exist. This would make essence and existence incomplete beings like prime matter and substantial form, which together make one complete being. But if there is only one complete being, the Suarezians insist that there can be no real distinction between the being and itself.

It may be said in conclusion that the controversy is not so important as many of the defenders of the real distinction seem to consider it. No problem of any great importance rests on its solution. It seems to be more in the spirit of sound philosophy not to admit more than is required to explain the facts, for beings are not to be multiplied without necessity, especially when an explanation of their function becomes difficult and irksome. If the real distinction is not required for the defense of any important truth, as most admit it is not, then we ought to prefer the simpler solution. From the very definitions of the terms it seems clear that existence is a state of being and not a being in itself.

SUMMARY OF CHAPTER VII

1 Essence is that which makes a being to be what it is. The essence of a being is expressed by giving its proximate genus and specific difference. The essence is sometimes also called nature, quiddity, or substance, with some variety of the connotations of these terms.

2 Essence is of two kinds, physical and metaphysical. The physical essence is given by enumerating the physical parts as they exist concretely in nature. The metaphysical essence is composed of the metaphysical grades of being. Both the physical essence and the metaphysical essence are real, but in different orders.

3 Properties of the metaphysical essence are immutability, indivisibility, necessity, and eternity. They amount to this, that the essence of a being cannot be changed without changing the being, and that the essence is independent of time. Those attributes belong to essences then in a po-

tential and negative sense, not as they belong to God in an actual and positive sense. It should be noted that the possibles have the same attributes and in the same sense.

4 Existence is opposed to mere possibility. It is the state of a being by virtue of which it is present as an actuality, and not merely as a possibility. The problem of the distinction between essence and existence may be stated thus: Is the distinction between essence and existence in an actually existing being real or only mental with a foundation in reality? Arguments are given for both sides which are interesting and instructive. As for the rest, "*in dubiis libertas, in omnibus caritas.*"

CHAPTER VIII

THE ANALOGY OF BEING

IN a previous chapter we presented Aristotle's doctrine of act and potency, which offers a partial solution to the problem posed by pantheism and by which Aristotle refuted both Parmenides and Heraclitus. But the main problem remains for solution in this chapter. The pantheists maintain that being is infinite and that there can be no other being or beings because the infinite already contains all perfection and cannot be increased by any other beings. Therefore only the One exists, infinite and absolute. This is a strong and logical argument and serves to explain the appeal of pantheism throughout the ages. Thus for several centuries Christian philosophy was threatened by a Platonic form of pantheism, and in modern times it is threatened by a Hegelian form.

We admit that the multiplication of beings cannot add to infinite perfection, but we answer the problem with the doctrine of analogy. The infinite and the finite are not the same kind of being; the reality of the second is only analogous to that of the first, a shadow, as it were, of the real substance, not a being in exactly the same sense. Finite beings are nonetheless real and really distinct from the infinite. It is only by such a distinction that even a partial solution to the problem can be reached.

It is necessary to begin from the beginning by showing the difference between a transcendental concept like being and a universal one like substance. The first is not a genus, the second is. This indicates that the process of precision by which these concepts are arrived at must be different; the first is subjective, the second is objective. When we unite the concepts again the same thing holds true; thus the union of being and *per se* is subjective, and that of substance and corporeal is objective. This is the basis of the analogy of being because being as predicated of its divisions into opposites must be analogous—that is, partly the same and partly different. Finally, this is seen to apply also to the division of being into being of itself (*ens a se* or God) and being from another (*ens ab alio* or creatures).

The concept of being not a true genus

In the diagram on page 16 substance and accidents are placed beneath being as two of its supreme divisions. This does not mean, however, that being is like the other concepts in that diagram, a genus which has two different species under it. A species is the result of the composition of a genus and a specific difference, two objectively different concepts. A specific difference is an essential note, new and extraneous to the content of the genus, not contained in its comprehension. For instance, materiality or corporeality is not contained in the idea of substance, but constitutes a true specific difference for it; it is an idea which adds something to the idea of substance which was not there before. Is this also true of the idea of being with reference to the idea *per se* or *standing by itself,* which when added to it gives us the idea of substance? From what we have said in Chapter 2 it should be clear that nothing outside the concept of being is added to it. *Per se* or the quality of standing by itself is also a being, and therefore one kind of being is added to another, but both are beings. This can be proved from an examination of either idea, that of genus or that of specific difference.

A genus cannot be formally predicated of one of its differences; for instance, it is not true to say that animality is rationality. But the idea of being, since it is transcendental in its extension, can be formally predicated of all things which distinguish one being from another; for example, the quality which changes the concept of being into the concept of substance is a being. If it were not a being, it would be nothing and it could not add anything to being considered simply as being; there would, therefore, be no change from the original concept.

A specific difference must be outside the essence of its genus; for instance, rationality must be outside of and different from animality. But no difference can be found outside the concept of being because outside of being there is only nothing or nonbeing. Thus there can be no difference which is not a being of some kind and therefore already contained in the idea of being in general. Being, then, is not a true genus and can have no true specific difference, precisely because it is a transcendental concept. No being is outside of it and all being is covered by it.

The composition of being

As was explained in Chapter 2, the idea of being is arrived at by a process of subjective precision because the ideas prescinded are only subjectively different; the difference is brought about by the action of the mind in producing now an indeterminate concept, *being,* and again a clear concept, *substance.* In the process of precision the differentiating characteristics are left out of account and the indeterminate idea of *being in general* is formed.

By composition in general is meant the union of elements that are distinct. The process of composition is exactly the opposite of the process of precision. It is a question of building up, of compounding or composing. Thus, various ideas may be added to the idea of being in order to arrive at more determinate concepts. For example, the idea of "standing by itself" may be added to the idea of being, thus forming the idea of substance. The difference existing between precision and composition may perhaps be clarified by the diagram on page 95. Note that precision, as indicated by the arrow in the diagram, is to be read from the bottom upward, while composition is to be read from the top downward.

Composition, like precision, may be either objective or subjective, depending on whether the ideas are objectively different or whether they include each other implicitly. The composition of animal and rational to form the idea of man is an objective one, just as the precision was objective. The composition of being and "standing by itself" to form the idea of substance is a subjective one, just as the precision was subjective. Some authors use the term *metaphysical composition* to describe objective composition, which unites ideas that are objectively different.

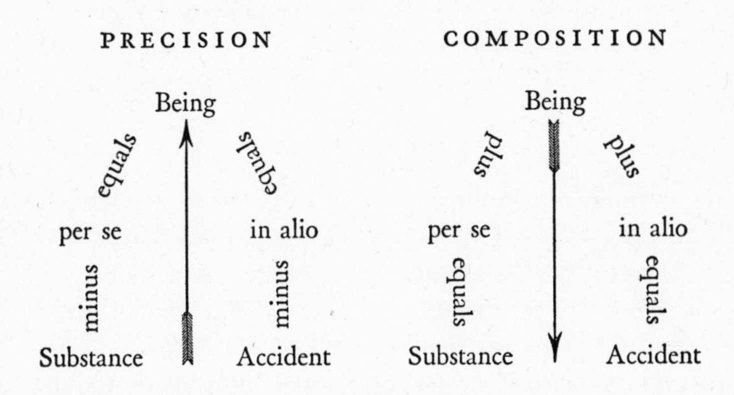

These same authors speak of *logical composition* when they are referring to the union of ideas which are only subjectively different; that is, they are different in the sense that the one idea (being) contains implicitly and vaguely what the other (substance) expresses explicitly and determinately.

The result of composition is an explicit and determinate kind of being; the idea of being in general is an implicit and vague expression of the same reality. What the modal differences of being add to the concept of being is being of a certain kind. For example, the very obscurity or vagueness of the idea of being in general is the reason why it is possible to apply the concept of being to an accident as well as to a substance. When, however, a mode or determination of the idea of being is added to it, such as "standing by itself" to form the idea of substance, you get a clear idea. In the example given, the result of the added determination is a clear idea of substance, which of course cannot be predicated of an accident. Thus it can readily be seen that the extension of the term *substance* is a contraction of the extension of the term *being.*

The analogy of being

By saying that the idea of being is predicated of its supreme divisions in a univocal sense, ontologists and pantheists in general confuse the infinite with the finite. It is not difficult to refute their error. The idea of being in general is not the same as the idea of the infinite being, God, because the idea of being in general is only an abstract and indeterminate concept, while the idea of the infinite is that of the *actus purus, ens perfectissimum,* or *plenitudo essendi* with no mixture of potentiality (potential being as well as actual being is included under the idea of being in general). Moreover, the infinite being must have concrete and actual physical existence, for the infinite being is the *ens necessarium;* the idea of being in general is only an idea, having reality only in the metaphysical order.

It is also possible to approach the matter in another way; that is, from the manner of predication of the idea of being of its inferiors or divisions, one of which is, of course, the division into God and creature *(ens a se, ens ab alio).*

Terms, which stand for ideas, may be of three kinds with regard to their meaning and predication. A univocal term is one which is predicated of several things in exactly the same sense: the term *man* is applied to Peter and Paul in exactly the same sense, rational animal; the term *animal* as applied to a man and a horse has exactly the same meaning, sentient living being. An equivocal term is one that is used of several things in an entirely different sense: the term *pen,* for example, could refer to an instrument for writing and to an enclosure for pigs; the term *page,* to a leaf in a book or to an attendant for some official. An analogous term is one which is predicated of different things in a sense which is partly the same and partly different: the term *healthy* can be applied to a man and to the medicine which a man takes to restore his health. The sense in this case would be partly different because health is really a quality of the man and is predicated of the medicine only because it may be a cause of health in the man. It should be clear that a term is not always used in the same way: if the term *pen* were to be applied to two instruments for writing, the term would be univocal in spite of all accidental differences that might exist between the two pens.

An analogous term, then, is midway between a univocal term and an equivocal term. It is based on a relation which the two things concerned have to each other, as medicine to the health of the man to whom it is given or as a scene that is said to be joyful has to the persons who feel joy. The terms do not mean two entirely different things, but the signification of one has a connection with the signification of the other.

What is the nature of the term *being* as it is predicated of its supreme divisions, substance and accident, God and creature, the absolute and the relative? It is obviously not equivocal; for in all these things, no matter how they differ among themselves, the essence of being is verified: they are all beings of some sort in that they are either existing or existible.

Is the term *being,* then, applied to each of its divisions in a univocal manner? Let us use substance and accident as an example and consider whether or not being can be predicated of them univocally. For a term to be univocal it is not sufficient that the same essence or thought content be present in both members of which the predication is made. That is undoubtedly true of the concept of being with reference to a substance and an accident. It is further required that this essence or thought content be present in both members in exactly the same sense. This requirement is not fulfilled in the example under consideration. The essence expressed by the term *being* is found in the substance in an independent and absolute sense; it is found in the accident in a dependent sense and in a manner related to the substance. But the qualities by which substance differs from accident are also beings; otherwise they would not be able to determine the general concept of being to any particular kind of being. Therefore substance and accident agree in their being but they differ in the *manner* of their being, which is also a being. The concept as applied to them is therefore partly the same and partly different. But this constitutes an analogy. Therefore the term and the concept *being* are used analogously when predicated of substance and accident.

It is of course clear, as Suarez is careful to point out, that the term *being* need not always be used analogously. When predicated of two substances, of two accidents, of two creatures, or even of two persons of the Blessed Trinity, it would be a univocal concept since it would apply to each of the two in exactly the same sense.

The analogy of the concept of being is dependent on the obscure and indeterminate nature of this concept. An example may help to make this fact clear. The term *animal* is a univocal term as applied to man and to the brute animal. Man and brute are animals in exactly the same sense; they are both sentient, living beings. They do indeed differ but not in the concept animal; the element in which they differ, rationality, is something entirely outside the concept of animal and is added to it as an objectively different concept. But in the case of the concept of being it is otherwise. The concept of being is that in which substance and accident agree and that in which they differ, because being is in everything and everything is a being. The reason why being is not a genus, why it is subjectively prescinded and subjectively put together again, is also the reason why the term and concept are analogous. Being is an obscure and indeterminate concept; substance, for example, is its clear and determinate expression.

Logical composition, or subjective composition, as we prefer to call it, is simply the clear expression of a reality which in the idea of being was expressed by a vague and obscure concept. The very obscurity of the concept of being is the reason why the concept can be applied to both members of the division of being into substance and accident. When, on the other hand, the idea of substance is expressed clearly by the union of the concepts of being and "standing-by-itself" to form the idea of substance, the new concept *substance* is really contracted in extension compared to the previous concept *being*.

Analogy is of two different kinds, that of proportion and that of attribution. Some authors maintain that the analogy of being is an analogy of proportionality; others hold that it is an analogy of intrinsic attribution. We will follow the teaching of Suarez on this point.

There is an analogy of proportion when the same term is applied because of a similarity in the two objects to which it is applied; for example, a meadow may be spoken of as smiling, a smiling meadow, because there is a kind of similarity to the smile on the face of a human being.

The word attribution is used in speaking of the second kind of analogy because the common essence is attributed to both objects. It is attributed only because it is really possessed by both objects; otherwise the attribution would be a false one. An analogy of attribution, therefore, exists when the essence is in both objects to which it is applied, intrinsically, but it is in the first primarily and perfectly and in the second with dependence on the first, and therefore imperfectly and relatively.

Two conditions, therefore, are required for an analogy of intrinsic attribution: first, the common essence must be in both objects in a true sense; second, it must be in the first object in an absolute and independent sense and in the second in a derived, dependent, and imperfect manner. But it is obvious from what has been said that this is true of the concept of being with regard to the finite and the infinite, substance and accident, the absolute and the relative. The term *being* applies to each one in a true and genuine sense; they are all beings of some sort. But it applies to the infinite in an absolute and independent manner; to the finite only in relation to and with dependence on the infinite. Substance also has being primarily and independently; accidents have being only with dependence on a substance. So, too, the absolute has independent being while the relative can exist only with dependence on the absolute. Being, then, while it is in each member of these divisions, is in them in a different manner. We say, then, that being belongs to them analogously, by an analogy of intrinsic attribution.

This problem of the analogy of the concept of being lies at the root of many other difficulties in philosophy. It is the same as the famous problem of the one and the many. If the concept of being is perfectly one—one in the univocal sense, as the idea of the universal is, for example—then we are placed in a real dilemma. We must admit that this univocal concept either corresponds to all reality or it does not so correspond. In either case there are disagreeable consequences.

If the univocal concept of being does correspond to all reality, then all reality is one and we have pantheism. Pantheists reason thus: If God and all other things are being in the same sense, then we are all part of God, and therefore the same as God. If there is to be a difference, say they, then being must differ from being by something that is being or by something that is nonbeing or nothing. But it is impossible that being should differ from being by being. It would be absurd to say that the reason for their similarity is also the reason for their difference. They must, therefore, differ in something that is not being; but outside of being there is only nonbeing or nothing. Therefore there is no difference among beings; they are not many, there is only the One.

To take the other horn of the dilemma, if the univocal concept of being does not correspond to all reality, there can be no knowledge of reality, and we have skepticism. Skepticism follows because all knowledge is reducible to the objective idea of being and if this idea lacks validity, all knowledge is invalid. There is no recourse, then, but to deny the assumption upon which this reasoning is based and to insist that the concept of being as applied, for example, to God and creature or to substance and accident must be analogous.

It should be noted that the analogy of being does not destroy the unity of the concept of being in every sense. It does mean, however, that this unity must be imperfect, subjective, or logical and not perfect, objective, or metaphysical. If a clear concept of being (for example, substance) is opposed to the obscure or indeterminate one, it is no longer univocal but analogous because there is a similarity and a difference in the same concept of being. The concept of being, then, is univocal in the logical sense and analogous in the metaphysical and real sense *(logice unum, metaphysice analogum)*.

SUMMARY OF CHAPTER VIII

1 The concept of being is not a true genus. Substance and accident are supreme divisions of being, not true species of

a true genus. A species results from the union of a true genus with a true specific difference. But being is not a genus because it can be predicated of its differences, and it has no specific difference because nothing can be added to it that is not also a being and therefore contained in its extension. A real specific difference must be outside of the genus and add some new concept to it. But every specific difference must be a being of some sort, and would not be outside of the idea of being. The only thing, so called, outside of being is nothing, and nothing can add only nothing to being.

2 The composition of being is a subjective process. When we prescinded being in Chapter 2 we found that it could be done only subjectively; that is, not by abstracting one objectively different concept from another, but only in the sense that the one idea, *being,* contained implicitly and vaguely what the other idea—substance, for example—expressed explicitly and determinately. When, therefore, we put them together again (composition) the process is reversed, but it is the same kind of process, a subjective or logical one.

The process of the composition of being with the quality of "standing-by-itself" results in a contraction of the idea of being; that is, the idea of substance which results from the composition is contracted or narrower in extension than the original idea of being. The idea of being is of course changed into the idea of substance; it does not remain the idea of being if it is contracted. The reason why the process must be subjective or logical is that all of the modes or determinations of being are themselves beings and are already included in the idea of being in an implicit and indeterminate manner, even though they are not expressed or represented as determinate beings.

3 A univocal term is one that is applied to several things in exactly the same sense. An equivocal term is one that is applied to several things in an entirely different sense. An analogous term is one that is applied to two objects partly in the same sense and partly in a different sense. Being is an analogous idea.

4 Analogy is of two kinds, that of proportion and that of attribution. An analogy of proportion exists when there is a similarity in the two objects to which the term is applied. An analogy of attribution exists when the nature or essence is in both objects of which it is affirmed, but it is in one primarily and independently and in the other secondarily and dependently.

Being as applied to the infinite and to the finite, as applied to a substance and to an accident, is obviously not equivocal because they are all beings in a true sense; neither is it univocal because it does not apply to them in exactly the same manner as, for instance, animal does to its several species; but it is analogous with an analogy of intrinsic attribution because it really exists in each member of its subordinate divisions, but in the first in a primary and independent sense and in the others secondarily and with dependence on the first. The problem of the analogy of being is important because on its solution depends whether or not we can avoid pantheism and skepticism in philosophic thought. If all being were one in a perfectly univocal sense, then one or the other of these untenable theories would necessarily follow. All beings cannot, therefore, be one in the univocal sense but must be analogous in the manner explained.

CHAPTER IX

BEING AND UNITY

THE concept of being is transcendental. It covers all reality of whatever kind and excludes only *nothing* from its extension. We have frequently used two synonyms for being which are, therefore, also transcendental—thing *(res)* and something *(aliquid)*. There are three other transcendental concepts which are properties or attributes of being. They are *one, true,* and *good*. They are identical with the concept of being, but they are not identical among themselves. They express different attributes of being and are different in their comprehension. A being is said to be one according to its own nature; it is true with reference to the intellect of some other being; and it is good because it is the object of some will or appetite.

Some of the material in this section of metaphysics may at first sight appear to be simple and obvious, and there is danger that we might be led into underestimating its importance. This would be a serious mistake. Without a clear understanding of the concepts of unity, truth, and goodness much of philosophy would become unintelligible and errors of a serious nature would be almost certain to result.

The meaning of unity

A being is said to be one when it is undivided in itself, and as a consequence divided from every other being. If it is a simple being, it cannot be divided; if it is compound, the parts must be united; otherwise it would be two beings, not one compound being. In this sense every being is one, and unity or oneness is a transcendental property of being. Transcendental unity, then, is an attribute of being by which it is undivided in itself and divided from all other beings. It is to be distinguished from predicamental unity, which is the unity of some standard by which we may measure the quantity of other things. We call an inch, a yard, or a mile a unit even though it can be divided indefinitely.

Kinds of unity

Unity may be either real or logical. Real unity is the indivision of a thing in its being, independently of the mind. There is a real unity of *simplicity* when the indivision is such that the being does not consist of any parts into which it might be divided. It is indivisible both actually and potentially. Such is the essence of God, the soul of man, or any pure spirit. There is a real unity of *composition* when the being is not actually divided into the real parts of which it consists. It is actually united and only potentially divisible. Body and soul in a living man are real physical parts which are united in an organic unity of a substantial nature. Man is, therefore, a composite unit.

This unity of composition may be of three kinds, metaphysical, physical, or moral. It is *metaphysical* if the unit consists of some of the grades of being as metaphysical parts. Thus, man considered as a rational, sentient, living, material substance is a metaphysical unit. The unity is *physical* if it consists of actual physical parts which belong together by nature. For instance, man's body is composed of various physical parts joined together to form the whole. A *moral* unity is formed as the result of the agreement of free beings; for example, societies, states, and families are moral units. This is also called an organic unity because it is similar in many respects to a physical organism.

Logical unity is a product of the mind's activity in forming universal or transcendental ideas. The mind groups a number of things, individual in nature, into a class and unites them into a conceptual whole. The concept *man* is a conceptual whole of which individual men are considered as logical parts. Hence logical unity can be defined as the indivision of a universal idea considered as a conceptual whole of which the members are parts.

The aggregation of many units is called a multitude. Multitude is potentially infinite in the sense that no limit can be assigned to it beyond which a further extension could not be conceived. The possibles, for instance, are potentially infinite. When multitude is measured by unity, we have the concept of number. Number can never be actually infinite because the very idea of number is that it should be measured by unity. It can be potentially infinite, as has been pointed out, but the concept of an infinite number or an infinite series actually existing is a contradiction in terms.

Being and one are convertible

When we say that being and unity are convertible we mean that every being is a unit or one, and that everything that is one or a unit is a being. The truth of this statement is almost self-evident. Every being is either simple or compound in its nature. These terms are contradictories: a being is compound when it consists of parts; it is simple when it does not consist of parts. Between contradictories there is no middle, and therefore every being must be either simple or compound. Now, whatever is simple is actually as well as potentially indivisible because it has no parts into which it might be divided; a simple being, then, must be undivided in itself and therefore a unit or one. Whatever is a compound being is a compound only insofar as its parts are united and not divided; therefore a compound being is undivided in itself and hence a unit or one. Every being, then, whether simple or compound, must be undivided and therefore a unit or one.

The converse of the proposition, that everything which is a unit is a being, is even more obvious. To be a unit means to have the unity of simplicity or of composition. But this necessarily presupposes something that has this unity. The concept of unity of composition applies to a reality consisting of parts, and the concept of unity of simplicity applies to a reality consisting of no parts. In both cases if there were no being or reality, there would be nothing; and nothing cannot be a unit of either kind, simple or compound. Hence only a reality, a being, can be a unit. Being and unity, then, are convertible: every being is a unit, and every unit is a being.

The nature of individuality

There is a special kind of unity called the unity of individuality or the unity of an individual. It may be defined as the unity of a being which is one in itself and not multipliable. The concept of the individual is thus seen to be in opposition to the concept of the universal. The universal is conceived by the mind as a nature common to many, capable of being realized in any number of individuals of that class. It is a logical or conceptual unit which as a class nature is communicable to many and therefore multipliable to the members of the class. The individual nature is conceived as being for itself alone and incommunicable to others, although there may be many others of the same class; that is, they may be the same specifically but are not the same numerically.

Plato erroneously held that universals exist concretely in the physical world and not merely as ideas. Why was Plato in error? Why is it that a being, if it exists, must exist as an individual and not as a universal? The answer is derived from the nature of the universal idea. It is a concept which applies to a class as a whole and to every member of the class. It is applicable to one and to many.

In the mind the idea itself is one, although it can be referred to many in reality; the thing as it exists in nature is one and individual, although it forms the basis of the universal concept which is formed by the action of the mind abstracting the common essence which is applicable to many. In the mind the objective concept of the universal is one in act, many in potency *(unum actu, plura potentia);* and in the real order it is many in act, one in potency *(plura actu, unum potentia)* by which is meant that the mind can form a universal concept which applies to many individuals in reality. It is, then, one and many under different aspects or in different orders, the physical and the metaphysical. It could not be both in the same order because that would violate the principle of contradiction. The doctrine of Plato that it is one and many in the same physical order is therefore contradictory. It has been proved in the preceding section that in the order of existing things every being is one. Consequently every being must come into existence as an individual and cannot be universal.

The principle of absolute individuation

Individuality is not communicable but is absolutely restricted to the individual. It can be defined as the state of an existing being in virtue of which it is one and not multipliable. This brings us to the problem of what it is that makes a being an individual in this sense. In other words, what is it in the being itself that makes it be this particular individual? Since this question refers to the single individual taken absolutely, the principle which gives the unity of individuality to an existing being is called the principle of absolute individuation.

The individual nature must be distinguished from the specific nature. The specific nature is the same as the definition; that is, the union of the proximate genus and the specific difference as, for example, in the definition *Man is a rational animal.* The specific nature must be alike in all men. In an existing man, however, this specific human nature becomes an individual human nature, and this takes place through some kind of union of the specific nature with the individuality.

The question, then, is: *What is the principle of absolute individuation which makes an individual be an individual?* There are two answers that are commonly given, although others have been proposed. It is either (1) a distinct entity called the entity of individuality or (2) the specific nature or essence itself which accounts for individuality. The answer to the question depends on the distinction which is held to exist between the two. If the individuality is an entity really distinct from the specific nature, then it is by that entity that the being is individuated. But if the individuality is only mentally distinct from the specific nature, then the two are really the same, there is no added entity, and the principle of individuation in that case would be the specific nature or essence itself. We maintain that there is only a mental distinction between the two and that, therefore, the principle of absolute individuation is the specific nature or essence itself. This we shall now proceed to prove.

If there were a real distinction in an existing being between its specific nature and its individuality, it would mean that the individual nature results from a physical composition of these two entities so that the specific nature, when it exists, could not become an individual nature except through this entity of individuality. But this existing specific nature in itself must be either universal or individual. If it is universal, then a universal would exist as universal in the physical order. But it has already been proved that this doctrine of Plato violates the principle of contradiction. Therefore the specific nature must come into existence as an individual nature. But if this is so, then the entity of individuality is useless because the specific nature is already an individual nature when it comes into existence. Therefore the individuality of an existing nature is not really distinct but only mentally distinct from the existing nature itself, and the principle of absolute individuation must as a consequence be the nature or essence itself. Accordingly it must be true that every specific nature by the mere fact that it exists becomes an individual nature. There is, then, no physical entity of individuality that is added to the nature, but individuality is a necessary manner of existence for a being in the physical order.

Between the specific nature and the individuality of an existing individual there is, then, only a logical or mental distinction. There is an obvious difference in concept because we do not mean the same thing when we speak of nature and of individuality. The precise nature of this distinction will be discussed more fully in the next chapter, but we may say here that according to most authors it is a distinction with an imperfect foundation in things. The foundation consists in this, that individuality is conceived as being the same in nature or kind for all individuals, but there is a great variety of specific natures, each of which is individuated in a large number of existing individuals. The two things are one in nature but are conceived differently by the mind, and there is a foundation in things for these different concepts.

The principle of relative individuation

In the previous discussion we have been considering the problem of absolute individuation, what it is that makes an individual be an individual, this individual thing. Now we shall consider the problem of relative individuation, what it is that makes it possible to have a number of individuals of the same species; for instance, why there can be many individual beings all of whom belong to the same species, man.

St. Thomas and Thomists generally answer the previous problem and the present one in the same way. For them the principle of absolute and relative individuation is the same thing, *materia quantitate signata,* matter as affected by quantity. One might think that all matter was necessarily affected by quantity, but St. Thomas speaks thus to distinguish actual matter from prime matter *(materia prima)* considered in the abstract. Thomists state the problem thus: It is a question of the plurality of individuals in the same species; the principle of relative individuation, then, must be a principle of plurality. Plurality, they say, implies divisibility. In the physical order the ground or principle of divisibility is matter affected by quantity because matter alone is divisible in such a manner that a plurality of individuals can arise out of its division. If one portion of matter is separated from another, there arises a plurality of beings in the same species. A very little reflection will make it clear that this is obviously true of all beings that are even partially material.

The opinion explains plurality in the world of sense, but we know that there are also spiritual beings. How does this theory apply to them? It is an obvious consequence of this doctrine that spiritual beings could not be multiplied in the same species but that each would constitute a separate species. Apart from the fact that we are accustomed to think of such spirits as constituting only a limited number of different and distinct divisions, it is hard for the mind to understand why it should be impossible to have a number of spiritual beings within the same species. There is certainly no contradiction in the idea. It appears that the Thomistic teaching on this point is rather weak and unnecessarily involved.

On these grounds Suarez and those who follow his line of thought offer a different explanation of the problem of relative individuation. They explain the principle of relative individuation as grounded in the contingency and finiteness of creatural beings. The infinitely perfect essence of God cannot be duplicated; there can be but one God. On the other hand, this is obviously not true of any creature. Creatures always remain finite both in essence and existence, and therefore they would seem to be multipliable both in species and number in any species without any limit as to that number. The reason is simple. God's essence is infinite and imitable. It is therefore potentially infinite in its imitability in any form. There is no reason to limit its imitability within a species any more than there is to limit the number of species. God's essence is actually infinite as an existing reality; therefore the possibility of its further imitability can never be exhausted. This applies to spiritual as well as to material beings; there is no difference between them as finite and contingent entities. These qualities, then, are the foundation or principle of their possible multiplicity within a species, the principle of relative individuation.

SUMMARY OF CHAPTER IX

1 There are three different properties or attributes of being which are necessarily connected with being but which are not explicitly contained in its concept as such. These are the attributes of unity, truth, and goodness.

A being is one when it is undivided in itself and divided from every other being. This is transcendental unity. It must be distinguished from predicamental unity, the unity of a standard for measuring quantity, such as a yard or a mile.

2 **Kinds of unity.** Unity is either real or logical. Real unity is the indivision of a being in its entity, independently of the action of the mind. Real unity is the unity of simplicity when the being has no parts into which it could be divided. It is the unity of composition when the being has real parts but they are actually united. Unity of composition is metaphysical when the parts are the metaphysical grades of being; it is physical when the parts united are physical parts; and it is moral when the union is formed as the result of an agreement among free beings.

Logical unity is the indivision of an idea representing a class and considered as a conceptual whole of which the members are the logical parts. It is a unity which the mind forms on account of a common essence in nature.

3 **Being and unity are convertible.** This means that every being is one and everything that is one is a being. Every being has either the unity of simplicity or the unity of composition. If it is simple, it cannot be divided and is therefore one. If it is a compound being, it is actually united and only potentially divisible. If it were actually divided, then it would be not one being but two or more. Everything that is one is a being because if it were no being, nothing, it could not be said to be one.

4 **The nature of individuality.** Individuality is a special kind of unity by virtue of which a being is one in itself and not multipliable. The individual is opposed to the universal idea or concept which represents a nature common to many. If the universal idea could exist as a universal physical thing, it would be both one and many in the same order, the physical order, which would violate the principle of contradiction. The doctrine of Plato to the effect that universals exist in the physical world is, therefore, false; a being can exist in the physical order only as an individual.

5 **The principle of absolute individuation.** This is the ground or reason which makes an individual be an individual. There are two possibilities considered: the physical entity of individuality, and the nature or essence of the being itself. The decision as to which it is depends on the nature of the distinction between the essence and the individuality in an existing individual. If they are really distinct, then the principle of absolute individuation is the entity of individuality. If they are only logically distinct, then it is the nature or essence itself. The distinction must be mental or logical because the specific nature cannot exist as a universal; if it exists, it must exist as an individual nature. The

principle of absolute individuation, then, must be the nature itself.

6 **The principle of relative individuation.** The problem is to determine the reason for the possibility of the existence of a number of individuals in the same species. St. Thomas Aquinas and Thomists generally answer this and the previous question in the same way. They say it is matter affected by quantity *(materia quantitate signata)*. Suarez and others explain it more simply by placing the reason in the finiteness and contingency of all created beings, material and spiritual alike.

CHAPTER X

IDENTITY AND DISTINCTION

THE nature of identity and distinction is one of the most important and fundamental points in philosophy; an accurate understanding of identity and distinction is essential to clear thought on almost any problem. Without such an understanding there can be no precision or consistency in a philosophical system.

The terms identity and distinction can be defined in a preliminary way by saying that identity is the sameness of concepts or things, whereas distinction is the absence of sameness between concepts or things. We have already given many examples of identity and distinction. To give just one illustration, we have just finished a discussion about unity as a transcendental attribute of being and have reached the conclusion that being and unity are convertible; every being is one, and everything that is one is a being. In reality, then, they are identical, but there is a distinction between them in thought.

In the sections that follow we shall outline the scholastic doctrine on identity and distinction, a doctrine that is commonly agreed on by Thomists and Suarezians alike. Then we shall explain briefly how the doctrine of the Scotists differs from the general doctrine. Finally, we shall offer a possible solution of the problem which may not be altogether devoid of merit. That the problem remains it is difficult to deny. In spite of all the scoffing at the Scotistic doctrine, especially in modern times, it is still upheld by a large and able group. No one can delude himself into thinking that the issue is settled as long as this remains the case.

Real identity and logical identity

Real identity is the unity of things in themselves. We have had several examples of this already. Being and unity are one in reality; they are different concepts in the mind.

A real identity is *metaphysical* when a being is one in such a way that it cannot change in any manner. God is the only being metaphysically identical with Himself.

There is real *physical* identity when a being is one in such a manner that it does not change in its essential reality. Such is any simple being; for example, the soul of man or a pure spirit possesses physical identity.

A real *moral* identity exists when any change in the essential nature of a being is successive and gradual. The human body is morally identical throughout life in spite of all the changes which take place in it.

Logical identity is the unity that exists among things which correspond to the same concept in the mind.

Things agree in some element, and the mind by reason of this agreement groups them under one concept and regards them as identical in this respect. Such things are distinct in reality but united in the same concept. Their point of similarity may be in their essence or their accidents.

An essential logical identity is based upon the sameness of the essence of things. Peter and Paul, James and John, all agree in possessing the same human essence.

An accidental logical identity is based upon agreement in the possession of accidents. Two men having a ruddy complexion are identical in that quality.

Real distinction

A distinction is real when it is made between beings that differ in their reality, independently of the action of the mind. Such a distinction may be either major or minor.

A major real distinction exists when things are distinct from each other as entities. The distinction may be between substances or accidents so long as the being of one is not the being of the other.

A minor real distinction exists between a thing and its mode. A mode is of such a nature that it confers no new reality upon its substance; the substance can exist without the mode, but the mode cannot exist apart from its subject. For example, there would be a minor real distinction between John and John's sitting on a fence.

As we have seen from past discussions, it often becomes important to differentiate between a real distinction and a logical distinction. The distinction is real when one or more of the entities are preserved in existence after they have been separated; when they are related as cause and effect or at least as principle and the things which flow from it; or when there is a difference of concept so that they imply incompatible elements, such as matter and spirit, substance and accident.

Logical distinction

A logical or mental distinction is a distinction between concepts which express the same reality. There are two kinds of logical distinctions, those without a foundation in reality and those with a foundation in reality. A distinction between concepts having one and the same reality without any foundation in the object itself for making the distinction is called a purely mental distinction. Logical distinctions with a foundation in reality are subdivided into those with a perfect foundation in reality and those with an imperfect foundation.

In the first kind the distinction is due entirely to the distinguishing power of the mind without any foundation in things. It is a purely mental distinction. Examples are terms and ideas which are synonymous in meaning, such as six and half a dozen, a ton and two thousand pounds. Other examples are the subject and predicate of a definition and the distinction between the transcendentals, being, thing, and something *(ens, res, aliquid)* which are pure synonyms.

In the logical distinction with a perfect foundation in things, the concepts are distinct from each other in such a way that they are objectively different in content even though they apply to the same physical reality. These concepts are not mutually inclusive; each has a definition different from the others. An example would be the metaphysical grades of being on the Porphyrian tree (page 16) as applied to man. Five objectively different concepts are applied to the same physical reality, man. He is a rational, sentient, living, material substance. These grades of being are properly distinguished from each other because they can be and actually are separately realized in other beings. We have, then, a reason or foundation for making a distinction between these five different concepts in the essence of man. Thus, as has been said, there is a logical distinction with a perfect foundation in reality when the mind forms objectively different concepts of the same physical reality and these concepts have as their foundation in reality the fact that they are objectively different concepts and can be separately realized in other beings, although in the individual being they stand for one physical reality.

A logical distinction with an imperfect foundation in reality is a distinction in which the different concepts that are applied to the one reality are not objectively different but include each other implicitly. Such a distinction exists between the concept of being and its supreme divisions, as has been explained previously. The idea of being in general includes everything that is not nothing; hence it embraces every reality, including substance, life, body, sentiency, and rationality. All of these things are also being and, therefore, include the idea of being implicitly.

The attributes of God provide another example of the logical distinction with an imperfect foundation in reality.

The distinction among any of God's attributes is one with only an imperfect foundation. The foundation is imperfect because God in His infinite perfection possesses a perfect unity of simplicity. He has no physical or metaphysical parts into which He could be divided. In creatures the concepts of wisdom, mercy, and justice are objectively different and can be separately realized, but this is not true of the infinitely perfect being. Each attribute of God is really identical with all others and with His essence, and a plurality of infinite perfections separately realized would be a contradiction in terms. The foundation for the distinction is in God only in the sense that He includes all the perfections of creatures in His infinite essence.

A third instance of this distinction which deserves to be noted is the distinction between the transcendentals, being, one, true, and good. All these concepts are convertible, as we have already shown with regard to unity. The concepts, however, do not mean the same thing, and the distinction between them is not without some foundation. Nevertheless each contains the others implicitly, and they cannot be separately realized. The distinction, therefore, is one with an imperfect foundation in reality.

The Scotistic division of distinctions

John Duns Scotus (1266-1308), founder of the later Franciscan school of philosophy, is famous for his sharp distinction. There is a good deal of dispute even among his followers as to the exact meaning of much of what he said, but it seems fairly certain that the only point of dispute between him and St. Thomas in this particular matter was the nature of the distinction which we have called logical with a perfect foundation in reality. Scotus admitted the other distinctions, and he did not wish to introduce a new one. He merely wished to define more accurately the one we have mentioned. He gave it the name of distinction *formalis a parte rei,* which we translate into English literally, *formal on the part of the thing.* It is really remarkable how many different interpretations have been given to these simple words. These opinions make up an instructive page in the history of philosophy.

In order to explain this distinction, "formal on the part of the thing," Scotus used the same example which had served St. Thomas to illustrate his logical distinction with a perfect foundation in the thing. It was the concepts of animal and rational in man or any grades of being in the Porphyrian tree. Scotus says that they are completely different concepts or formalities; they are objectively different antecedently to the action of the mind *(a parte rei);* they can be and actually are separately realized in other beings. They cannot, then, be called only logically distinct, since they are distinct *a parte rei.* If we look back to St. Thomas' logical distinction with a perfect foundation, we shall see that he admits that the distinction has an antecedent and independent foundation in reality. He used the words *objectively different* and *perfect foundation in reality*. But that and nothing else is exactly what Scotus meant by the expression *formalis a parte rei,* which we can now translate as formally objective, or perfectly objective, which St. Thomas did not deny but on the contrary emphatically asserted.

Before proceeding further in this controversy let us examine the kinds of distinction advocated by each party in order to have the matter more clearly in mind. We shall arrange the different distinctions in logical order according to their reality or nearness to reality.

THOMISTS		SCOTISTS	
Real		Real	
Logical	with perfect foundation	Formal	*(realis secundum quid)*
	with imperfect foundation	Logical	with foundation *in re*
	with no foundation (verbal)		with no foundation

We see a great similarity in these outlines. The only difference is the distinction which according to St. Thomas approaches nearest to reality and which Scotus calls *realis secundum quid;* that is, real in a broad sense. One says it has a perfect foundation in reality; the other says that it obtains independently of the mind's action. Is there anything but a verbal difference between these statements?

There are different schools of thought among Franciscan scholars as to the proper interpretation of the formal distinction of Scotus.[1] The opinion here expressed by the author is substantially the same as that held by the first and larger school of Scotistic thought and is in our judgment only verbally different from that of the second

[1] These are explained fully and accurately by Maurice J. Grajewski in *The Formal Distinction of Duns Scotus* (Washington: Catholic University of America Press, 1944). Consult also Gerard Vogt, "Note on the Formal Distinction of Scotus," *Franciscan Studies* 3:40-41, August 1925.

school. It is certainly not a new interpretation, as is apparent from a study of the literature on the subject. The opinion is also that of Father Joseph Hontheim, S.J., given in his *Theologia naturalis,* which we have presumed to follow.[2]

We submit that both sides appear to have forgotten that they have been teaching that there are two kinds of reality, physical and metaphysical, or actual and possible. It should be obvious that the Thomistic logical distinction with a perfect foundation in reality and the corresponding Scotistic distinction *formalis a parte rei* are both founded in metaphysical reality as explained in their own words. A man, if he exists, has one physical reality; and whether he exists or not, his essence is composed of five metaphysical realities or grades of being. This being the case, we submit the following diagram which in our opinion explains clearly what both parties to the dispute wish to say. We shall also give the examples which they themselves gave to illustrate each division.

DISTINCTIONS

Real	physical—James, John
	metaphysical—animal, rational
Logical	with a foundation in reality—being, substance
	with no foundation in reality—six, half dozen

The truth of the diagram is evident from the doctrine in the previous pages concerning being and its precision and composition; concerning the possibles, their nature, and ultimate ground; and concerning the reality and na-

[2] Joseph Hontheim, *Theodicea, sive theologia naturalis,* pp. 72 ff., *passim.* Fribourg: Herder and Company, 1926.

ture of the metaphysical order. The whole controversy might be reduced to a simple question: Is there a metaphysical order? If there is not, then Aristotelianism and scholasticism both fall together. But the answer to the question of course is yes; and both St. Thomas and Scotus himself defend it in countless places.[3]

SUMMARY OF CHAPTER X

1 **Real identity.** Identity in general is the sameness of concepts or things, whereas distinction is the absence of sameness of concepts or things. Real identity is the sameness of things in themselves, independently of the mind. It is metaphysical when the thing cannot change in any manner. It is physical when the thing cannot change in its essential reality. It is moral when the change which takes place in the being is successive and gradual.
2 **Logical identity.** This is the sameness that exists among things which correspond to the same concept in the mind. It is an essential logical identity when the sameness is one of essence. It is an accidental identity when the sameness is in accidents.
3 **Real distinction.** This is the absence of sameness between things different in their reality, independently of the mind. It is a major real distinction when the things differ to such an extent that they are distinct from each other as entities. It is a minor real distinction when things are distinct from each other as a being is distinct from its mode.

[3] The following references in St. Thomas are cited as examples: *In I metaphysicorum* 9, lect. 2; *Summa theologiae* I, q. 25, a. 3; *Contra gentiles* I, cap. 30, n. 21; *Summa theologiae* I, q. 15, a. 2. In the works of John Duns Scotus the following passages may be consulted: *Summa theol. opus oxon.* I, d. 2, q. 7, nn. 41 ss.; *Report. Paris.,* I d. 45, q. 2, nn. 5, 9.

4 **Logical distinction.** A mental or logical distinction is a distinction between concepts which express the same reality. It is a purely mental distinction when there is no foundation for it in reality. The logical distinction with a foundation in reality is of two kinds, according to the Thomistic school—one with a perfect foundation in reality, and the other with an imperfect foundation. That with a perfect foundation is exemplified by the distinction between the different metaphysical grades of being, such as animal and rational. The concepts are objectively different in content. The distinction with an imperfect foundation in reality is a distinction in which the different concepts that are applied to the one reality are not objectively different but include each other implicitly. An example would be the concepts of being and substance.

5 John Duns Scotus gave a different explanation of the nature of the distinction which other scholastics call logical with a perfect foundation in reality. He called it *formalis a parte rei, formal on the part of the thing,* objectively different independently of the mind. We believe that the difference is only in terminology and that both great men were trying to say the same thing; namely, that the distinction is a real metaphysical one. For example, man, if he exists, is one physically; but whether he exists or not he is a metaphysical multiplicity, being constituted of five different metaphysical grades, or essences, or possible beings.

CHAPTER XI

BEING

AND TRUTH,

GOODNESS, AND BEAUTY

UNITY is a transcendental attribute of being in general. Every being possesses this property absolutely and essentially; it would be a unit in itself even though no other being existed. Every being by its very nature also has a relation to intellect and will, by which it can be said to be true and good. These relations of truth and goodness are thus also transcendental for every being.

We come to know the nature of truth by observing our own mental operations. Truth is primarily the truth of thought. All truth must have a relation to an intellect; but that relation may be diverse, as we shall explain shortly. We shall consider later whether beauty is likewise one of the transcendental relations.

The will can desire something only insofar as it is known by the intellect as good; hence the relation of a being to the intellect, by which it is said to be true, is prior to its relation to the will. The truth of a being, therefore, is logically prior to its goodness, and for this reason we will discuss first the transcendental attribute of truth.

Nature and kinds of truth

Truth in general can be defined as the agreement between intellect and thing. There are two kinds of truth in this sense, the truth of thought and the truth of things. Both the truth of thought and the truth of things exist with regard to the human intellect, but they exist primarily and perfectly with regard to the divine intelligence. Falsity, of course, is the disagreement between intellect and thing.

When we speak of truth we usually mean the truth of knowledge or *thought,* the agreement of the intellect with the thing. This kind of truth is also called logical truth. It refers, not to ideas, but to judgments, which alone can be said to be formally true or false. The idea *man* and the idea *wise* cannot be said to be formally true or false; but when we enunciate the proposition, "The man is wise," then we have a judgment which must be either true or false. Thus the mind produces judgments which either do or do not correspond to reality. If the judgments correspond to reality, they constitute true knowledge; if they do not, we have logical falsity or error.

The truth of *things,* on the other hand, consists in the conformity of the thing with the intellect; it is known as ontological truth. The essences of things are modeled by the Creator upon perfections known to the divine intellect as existing in the divine essence. These essences, then, are ontologically true because they are in conformity with their exemplars in the divine mind. They may then be created by divine omnipotence and become ontologically true in the physical order.

We speak of true or false friends, of a true or real diamond, or a false or spurious one. If a thing conforms to our idea of what it ought to be, we call it true. We see, then that truth may be an attribute of things as well as of judgments. With reference to the human mind, however, ontological truth is only derived and secondary, although it is true that man can fashion things according to his own ideas and that they will then have ontological truth for him. Ontological truth refers primarily and intrinsically to the divine mind because ultimately it is their conformity to that mind that makes things ontologically true.

In addition to logical truth and ontological truth, there is also a third kind of truth, moral truth, which consists in the agreement of speech with thought. If there is no conformity between speech and thought, a lie or falsehood has been told. A person may be mistaken as to the real nature of things, but this does not affect the morality of his speech. As long as he speaks what is in his mind, he speaks the truth, no matter how far his words may be from the actual facts. The opposite is also true; if what he says is contrary to what he thinks, he tells a lie even though what he says may be in agreement with objective reality.

Each of these three kinds of truth receives special emphasis in a different branch of philosophy. Logical truth is treated in logic and epistemology. Moral truth is considered in the science of ethics. In metaphysics we are concerned primarily with ontological truth as one of the transcendental attributes of being.

The ultimate foundation of truth

As has already been pointed out, the mind possesses logical truth when the representation in the mind is in conformity with external reality. It is evident, then, that logical truth presupposes the being of the things known, for there could be no representation without something to be represented. Logical truth, therefore, has its foundation in the object known.

In the case of ontological truth there must be some type or standard in the mind to which a thing must conform in order to be true. It is evident that these type or pattern ideas, exemplars as they are called, are not to be found in a finite mind but must belong to a being who is responsible for the existence of their reality. Ontological truth consists in the reality of the things themselves, which must conform to the idea of them existing in that intellect whose essence is the ultimate foundation of their reality. This intellect can be no other than the divine mind. God created all things according to the exemplars which He had of them in His divine mind before creation. They were made in conformity with God's ideas of them, and in that their ontological truth consists. Ontological truth belongs to God's essence because His essence is in eternal conformity with His divine intellect; it belongs to possible as well as to actual being because the possibles too are in conformity with the exemplars which God has of them in His mind. Their reality depends on His essence; their ontological truth depends on His intellect. The ultimate foundation of all truth, then, is found in the conformity of all being with the divine mind.

Convertibility of being and truth

We have proved in a previous chapter that being and unity are convertible. The proof for the present proposition—that being and truth are convertible—is very similar. All finite beings, whether actual or potential, have reality because they are imitations of the essence of God. But in imitating His essence they necessarily imitate His ideas, since the two are perfectly identical on account of His nature as infinite perfection. Finite beings, therefore, have reality only by agreeing with the ideas of God. But to agree in their reality with God's ideas is to agree with His intellect; and that is the same as saying that they are ontologically true. We have already shown that God's essence is ontologically true; therefore all being is ontologically true, and ontological truth is a transcendental attribute of all being.

The proof of the proposition that everything that is true is a being is almost self-evident. Ontological truth is something. If it were nothing, it could not be an attribute of being. If it is not nothing, it must be a being. Consequently everything that is ontologically true is a being.

The meaning of falsity

We need scarcely insist on the existence of moral falsity; that is, of falsehood or lies. The existence of logical falsity or error is equally obvious. Is there, however, such a thing as *ontological* falsity? We have just shown that everything is ontologically true. In the absolute sense, therefore, and in relation to the divine mind, there can be no ontological falsity. But we may speak of ontological falsity relatively and with relation to the human mind. The result of man's labor does not always agree with the plan or idea he had in mind when he started it, and therefore it is ontologically false to some degree. In natural things, too, we are often deceived by false appearances and judge otherwise than according to fact. This is really logical falsehood, but we nonetheless speak of the *things* as being false. This is, however, only by extrinsic denomination. False diamonds are always true paste, false gold is true iron pyrites, false faces are true masks, and it is possible to know all of them for what they really are.

The properties of truth

Truth is primarily in the intellect. The truth of thought, then, or logical truth is the fundamental kind of truth. The word *truth* is applied in the first place to knowledge and judgments; it belongs to things only in a secondary and derived manner. Even when speaking of God, truth is predicated in the first place of His mind and not of His essence. It is attributed to reality only secondarily and analogically. The reality of things is the cause of logical truth in created minds. In the case of the divine mind things are made to conform to the exemplars existing therein, and by reason of this conformity are said to be ontologically true. Truth is primarily, therefore, an attribute of the intellect of God and only secondarily an attribute of things.

Truth is often spoken of as being eternal. In many senses, of course, truth is purely temporal; nevertheless, created truth, in spite of the fact that it is created, can be truly said to be eternal with a kind of extrinsic or negative eternity. Created things obviously do not possess any physical reality which is positively eternal, but they have a metaphysical reality which is eternally in conformity with God's knowledge of them, and their physical reality, if they have any, must therefore have had such conformity from eternity. Thus it is eternally true that man is a rational animal because he is a possible reality from all eternity, though man himself as a physical being is created and temporal.

In the same sense truth is said to be immutable. If a thing is eternally true, it must be immutably true. All created beings, whether possible or actual, are immutably true because they must always agree with God's knowledge of them.

In previous chapters we spoke of metaphysical essences and the possibles (which are also metaphysical essences) as being eternal and immutable in precisely the same sense as we speak of truth here. There is, then, nothing new in this doctrine; it is merely a corollary of several things that have been discussed previously.

Pragmatism

Pragmatism is a favorite doctrine in modern philosophy. Well-known philosophers, such as Hume, Locke,

Spencer, and Mill, have subscribed to its main teachings. In our own country one of its ablest exponents was William James. Pragmatism teaches that all truth is relative; that what is true today may be false at some other time; that what is true for one mind may be false for another. Let Professor James describe it in his own words. " 'The true,' to put it very briefly, is only the expedient in the way of our thinking, just as 'the right' is only the expedient in the way of our behaving."[1] And in another place: "True ideas are those that we can assimilate, validate, corroborate, and verify. False ideas are those that we can not. This is the practical difference it makes to us to have true ideas; that, therefore, is the meaning of truth, for it is all that truth is known as."[2]

James obviously denies that there is such a thing as absolute truth—truth that is the same for all minds, has its foundation in the necessary essences of things, and is ultimately conformed to the divine mind. According to him expediency is the measure of all truth. We have reason to be grateful to Professor James for his frank statement in this place, as in many others. Some of our adversaries make discussion difficult by their lack of candor and clarity. But such a criterion of truth obviously denies the existence of the supreme intelligence which is the measure of all truth and gives it its absoluteness, necessity, and eternity. If there is no such supreme intelligence, then the universe becomes irrational, and in that case expediency is perhaps as good a measure of truth as any other.

[1] William James, *Pragmatism,* p. 222. New York: Henry Holt and Company, 1892.

[2] *Ibid.,* p. 201.

But in that case truth has lost all its meaning and becomes simply that which is physically good for us here and now.

Truth and contingently future events

From what has been said previously we can understand that future events, since they will be true in the future, are true now and were true from all eternity in the sense that it is true now and was true from all eternity that they *will be* at this future time. This is of course obviously true with regard to events proceeding from necessary causes, such as the forces of nature. That there will or will not be a solar eclipse at a given time is already determined in its causes, and the fact is known to science. There can be no doubt about the truth of such future events, since they are the result of necessary causes. As such they are obviously known by God from all eternity; they can also be known by man while they are still only events that will happen in the future, insofar as their relationship to the necessary cause is recognized to exist, as in the case of the solar eclipse mentioned above.

The problem, then, concerns the truth and knowability of future events that are contingent; that is, events that do not proceed from necessary causes but rather follow from the decisions of the free wills of rational beings. Let us take an example. Here are two propositions: I shall play in the baseball game on Saturday; I shall not play in the baseball game on Saturday. Until the game has begun it is impossible for any man to say whether or not I shall actually play. Does this mean that neither of these propositions is true or false until after the game has started, and that therefore the free future does not now possess truth and intelligibility in itself?

Some philosophers assert that such contingent future events cannot be said to be true or false until the decision of the free will has been made. Others hold that one of these contradictory statements is true and the other false at all times, even from eternity, and that the free future is therefore an object of God's knowledge from all eternity. We agree with the latter opinion and submit three proofs in support of our position.

The first argument is based on the fact that the futurible, as it is called, is an object of knowledge—there is nothing in its nature that makes it unknowable as, for example, a square circle is unknowable. Beginning with this fact, then, we can proceed as follows to prove that God knows the free future.

Whatever has intelligibility or truth must necessarily be known from all eternity by God, who has infinitely perfect knowledge. But the free future has truth and intelligibility. Therefore it must be known by God from eternity. The major follows necessarily from the nature of God. The minor may be proved thus. If any free future ever happens, it was always true that this would happen. Therefore the proposition that a free act which at one time takes place, will happen, is true and an object of knowledge from eternity; accordingly the free act itself is true and knowable from eternity.

The second argument is from the nature of God's knowledge. God knows the free future when it takes place. But what God knows at any time He knows from all eternity, since His knowledge is immutable and since

God cannot ever receive any new perfection. Therefore God knows the free future from all eternity.

The third argument is drawn from the common consent of mankind. The very fact that man has always addressed prayers of petition to the supreme being is perhaps the most obvious indication that mankind acknowledges, not only that God knows the future, but that He is able to control it. That men accepted the words of the prophets as revelations of the future manifested by God through these intermediaries is another proof that men have always recognized the fact that God has knowledge of the free future.

As is apparent from the proof of the minor given in the first argument, we could prove also the eternal truth of God's knowledge of contingently future events by His knowledge of the possibles. For the futuribles as objects of knowledge are closer to reality than the possibles, since not only are they possible, but of two contradictory futuribles one will be actually true and the other actually false in the future. Therefore, if God knows the possibles, He knows the futuribles *a fortiori*.

The nature of goodness

Aristotle defined the good as "that which all desire." Desirability is, however, rather a property of the good than a real definition. The good might be described more accurately as that which is suitable to a natural inclination or desire. The good is desired because it satisfies some aptitude, tendency, or need of the particular being which strives after it. Each nature has its own needs and appetites, and whatever satisfies them will be good for that nature. This idea of good is fulfilled in three kinds of good, each somewhat different from the others.

Ontological good consists in the being or reality of the thing itself inasmuch as it represents the being, reality, and goodness of the infinite good, God. Every being, therefore, since it possesses being or reality, is ontologically good.

A thing is a physical good when it perfects the nature of a being. Each being has its own requirements according to its nature, and when these are fulfilled the being has acquired a physical good. All of man's powers, faculties, and parts are physically good for man. His sight, his hearing, his health, and his hair are all physically good for him.

An action is morally good when it is according to the moral order. An action might readily be an ontological and physical good and yet a moral evil. An example will make this clear. During the course of his lifetime a certain man kills two people. On the first occasion he kills in justifiable self-defense. On the second occasion he kills a man in the course of an attempt to rob that man. In both cases he kills a human person. In both cases his action, insofar as it is a being, is ontologically good. In both cases the action, insofar as it is well executed and successful, is a physical good. But the morality of the two actions is very different. In the first case the act is morally good because killing in self-defense is justifiable. In the second case the killing constitutes murder because it has no justifying reason. Thus an action may be both ontologically and physically good and yet be morally evil.

Other divisions of good which are of special importance in the science of ethics might also be mentioned. An *objective* good is anything that is good in itself. A *subjective* good consists in the possession of the objective good. God, for instance, is an objective good; our possession of Him would be a subjective good.

A good is *real* when it is considered to be a good for a being and actually is good for it. A good is *apparent* when it is thought to be a good but is really not good for the being. Pleasure is a real physical good, but excess in the use of it would be a moral evil, and therefore the particular pleasure involved would become only an apparent good. The pleasure would still be good in itself, ontologically and physically, but its abuse would be a moral evil. So it is with all God's gifts. We do not change their nature by our abuse of them. Man is both an animal and a spiritual being, and both elements must be considered in appraising what is good. Many things that are physically good must be regarded by man as apparent goods and not as real goods.

A *pleasurable* good is one which gives pleasure or enjoyment. A *useful* good is one which can be used as a means to another good. These goods do not need further explanations because their meaning is clear from the terms themselves.

Convertibility of being and goodness

Goodness is a transcendental attribute of being and as such is convertible with it; that is, every being is good, and whatever is good is a being. The proof is given by

St. Thomas in the following manner: "Every being, inasmuch as it is being, is in some way perfect, because every actuality is a certain perfection. But what is perfect involves the idea of appetible and good. Hence it follows that every being as such is good."[3]

To elaborate, we say that every being is good for itself. This may be proved syllogistically as follows: Good is that which is suitable and desirable for a thing; but nothing is more suitable and desirable for any being than its own nature; therefore every being is good for itself. Its own nature is the first essential perfection which any being has and it is therefore good for it.

Every being is also good for other beings. If it is good in itself, it can in some way be of help and add to the good of some other beings by communicating its goodness to them. This can be shown by examples of how one good helps to add its goodness to other beings. God, for instance, is the greatest good and the root of all other goods, communicating His goodness to all creation. Among finite beings accidents are a good for a substance, material substances are for the good of intelligent beings, and spiritual substances can help each other in various ways.

Goodness, then, is a transcendental attribute of being. Of what kind or kinds of goodness is there question in these proofs? Obviously they refer to ontological goodness in the first place, since all being and all goodness is but an imitation of the being and goodness of God. But it is almost equally obvious that they refer also to physical goodness because every one of the goods mentioned is also a physical good, including the nature or essence of a

[3] *Summa theologiae* I, q. 5, a. 3.

being. This is its first physical act or perfection, and therefore a good for the being and the foundation of all other good. In all physical beings, therefore, both ontological and physical goodness are convertible with being.

That whatever is good is a being is self-evident. The good cannot be nothing, for it is something which is suitable and desirable. *Nothing* could not be suitable or desirable. Therefore whatever is good is a being. The good is also convertible with reality and act in the sense of perfection.

The nature of evil

Evil is not a being; it is the absence of being. It is a defect, a privation of the perfection which belongs to a thing. It is defined as the privation of a required good *(privatio boni debiti)*. There are as many kinds of evil, so-called, as there are corresponding kinds of good. *Physical* evil is the privation of a physical good. Such would be the loss of a member of the body. The existence of such physical evils in the form of privations is obvious. *Moral* evil is the absence of a proper relation between a human act and its norm or criterion of morality. The absence of such order is also an obvious fact of life. In the matter of *ontological* evil, so-called, the answer is not so simple. We have just proved that every being insofar as it is a being is ontologically and physically good. If it is evil, it is because there is a privation of the good, a privative logical being or a nothing, a nonbeing. There can, then, be no ontologically evil being because every being, insofar as it has being, is good. What about a cancerous growth or the germs which are the cause of a disease? Even in these cases we say that the germs are good for themselves, and the cancerous growth has its own nature and that nature is good for it. Both things are in certain respects evil—they harm the body in which they reside, they constitute a lack of right order in a healthy body—but they are not evil in themselves and they can be a cause of good to other beings. Even the devil himself has a nature which is ontologically and physically good; in his case the evil consists in the deordination of a depraved will, forever opposed to the divine will.

False theories of evil

Pessimism is a philosophic theory which maintains that evil predominates over good, that the world at large is essentially bad. Life, it teaches, is not worth living; consciousness is a continual misery. Such is the main outline of the doctrine taught by Buddhism and the pessimism which has been defended in modern times by men like Schopenhauer, Hartmann, and Nietzsche.

No one denies that pain and suffering are physical evils; but they are not positive entities, as the pessimists maintain, but only privations in a being itself essentially good. Neither can it be denied that evils can be used to produce good of a higher order and that they can serve a purpose even on the physical plane. The world is not the best possible world that could have been created, but is limited in its perfections. Nevertheless it is ontologically and physically good and capable of attaining the purposes for which it was created.

Another false theory is excessive dualism, such as was taught in the sixth century B.C. by Zoroaster, a Persian philosopher. He held that there are two supreme principles in the world, the principle of good and the principle of evil. These two principles are in constant conflict for the mastery of the world. In the third century A.D. a variation of Zoroastrianism was introduced into Europe by Manes, the founder of the sect of the Manichees, of which St. Augustine was a member for many years. Manes taught that God was the principle of good and matter the principle of evil. In every theory of excessive dualism the error lies in conceiving evil as a positive entity instead of a privation of good, at least of that good which consists in proper order. The lack of proper order, whether it is the result of excess or the result of defect, is evil, both physical and moral. These errors affected not only philosophy but also the history of Europe; they formed the foundation for some of the gloomy and pessimistic theological doctrines that were formulated during the Protestant Revolt.

The nature of beauty

Beauty is closely connected with the good. In fact, St. Thomas says that they are really identical, although there is a logical distinction between them. He defines the beautiful as follows: *Those things are beautiful which please when seen.*[4] The definition makes clear that there are both subjective and objective elements in beauty. "Seen" of course means intellectual cognition rather than merely

[4] *Summa theologiae* I, q. 5, a. 4, ad 1.

sense knowledge, although that is also included, as we shall see presently.

Subjective elements in beauty

The pleasure derived from beauty is called aesthetic pleasure. The agreeable feeling which we have in the possession of something or the satisfaction of the lower appetites of man is not the enjoyment of beauty. This is a purely selfish and animal pleasure consequent on the satisfaction of an organic faculty. The enjoyment of beauty, whether in nature or art, is not selfish but disinterested. Aesthetic pleasure comes from beholding or contemplating the object without any desire of possession or of satisfaction other than that which comes to the mind through the senses. The eye, the ear, and the imagination are the sense faculties through which the perception of beauty is aroused in the mind.

It follows from the foregoing that the pleasure which beauty gives must be an intellectual pleasure. There is no indication among brute animals that they experience the joy in the beauty of nature which man feels, and this conclusion could also be reached from the fact that animals produce nothing that might cause the experience of beauty in other creatures. Only men are artists; animals do many clever things, but they produce nothing beautiful unless it is by a compulsion of their nature. Beauty appeals in the last analysis to the judgment of man, and judgment is an intellectual act. As we shall see presently, there is much beauty that can appeal only to the higher faculties of man.

The appeal of the beautiful, however, must be to the intellect through the senses. The idea must be clothed in a pleasing sensible appearance, for if there were no sensuous element, there would be no beauty. Abstract ideas are not beautiful. We have such ideas in the sciences, in mathematics, and in philosophy, and no one considers knowledge as such beautiful. It is the artist, and not the philosopher or the scientist, who gives us beauty. There is truth in what the artist portrays, but it must appeal to the senses in order to give aesthetic pleasure.

The reason for this is simple. Man is a compound being; he has mind and body, and both must be appealed to before he can enjoy the contemplation of beauty. There must be in the thing that we call beautiful a balance that takes into account the composite nature of man. If the object were too intellectual, there would be a lack of beauty, and if it were too sensuous, the pleasure it afforded would be mere sensible pleasure. In beauty there is one of the most obvious applications of the doctrine of the golden mean. Just as virtue stands midway between the evil of excess and the evil of defect, so beauty must not appeal solely either to the body or to the mind. This is really a result of our finite nature. Pantheism would naturally ridicule such a demand for moderation.

Finally, beauty is not a matter of the will but of the intellect. It is concerned, not with desire, but with cognition. The appeal of beauty is to the cognitive faculties of man. There may be desire aroused by the thing which is beautiful, but that is a consequence of beauty and not beauty itself. The understanding and appreciation of beauty gives aesthetic pleasure. The pleasure which comes from desire or the satisfaction of desire is not the joy which is aroused by beauty.

Objective elements in beauty

Unity, truth, and goodness are without doubt fundamental factors in beauty. Beauty and unity are closely related. If there is no unity in the thing contemplated, there can be no symmetry or harmony, and hence no beauty. Beauty comes from an orderly arrangement of parts, and such an arrangement gives unity to the whole. Beauty and truth are also related; in fact, one of the well-known definitions of beauty is the "effulgence of truth" *(splendor veri.)*. There must be truth before it can shine in splendor. This is understood from what has been said already to the effect that the appeal of beauty must be ultimately intellectual, for the intellect is the faculty for knowing truth. Beauty and goodness are still more closely related. The element of goodness must be present in the beautiful because beauty gives delight and pleasure, and these are the objects of desire or appetite, and therefore a pleasurable good. The pleasure is called forth by the presence of the objective good. There is, however, a difference between the good and the beautiful, at least in concept. The good satisfies by being acquired or possessed; beauty delights or gives joy without actual possession, merely by knowledge and contemplation. The joy that we feel in the good is a selfish enjoyment in many cases; the joy which beauty gives must be disinterested—that is, without any desire of acquisition other than through knowledge.

There must be unity, truth, and goodness in the beautiful, but it does not follow that beauty is therefore a transcendental attribute of being as the other three are. Beauty is not convertible with being or with any of its three attributes. It is true that everything that is beautiful is a being, one, true, and good, but everything that is good is not beautiful, at least not in the ordinary way that men speak of beauty. Only a small amount of being is really beautiful. No one thinks of calling an ordinary factory, or a barn, or a toad, or a mule beautiful. Being and beauty, or goodness and beauty, then, are not the same, and beauty is not a transcendental in itself or as synonymous with goodness.

St. Thomas enumerates three particular objective elements which must be found in a beautiful object. The first of these is integrity or completeness. The absence of a part which belongs to the nature of a being, a defect, or the mutilation of any part does not give pleasure, but produces an unpleasant impression upon the beholder. In such a case there is no rest in the enjoyment of beauty, but rather a feeling of irritation and annoyance. It may be in some cases that the defect is small and relatively unimportant to the object as a whole; in such an instance it could be overlooked, and the thing as a whole would still have the effect of giving pleasure to the contemplating mind. A noticeable defect, however, would tend to destroy the beauty of an object.

Proportion or balance is the second element noted by the Angelic Doctor. There must be an orderly and proportionate arrangement of parts; otherwise the object cannot give aesthetic pleasure. A pile of stones is not beautiful, but arranged as parts of a building the stones would take on balance and symmetry and hence could have beauty. As in architecture, so also in music and painting, the secret is in proportion, balance and symmetry, unity and variety. It is the balance and harmony of the one in the many that is capable of producing the pleasure characteristic of beauty.

St. Thomas mentions clarity or splendor as the third particular requirement for beauty. To be beautiful an object must be impressive, it must shine out in its splendor and clarity so as to force itself on the notice of the mind. It must be vivid and attractive in its presentation so as to appeal powerfully to the imagination of the beholder. It must be capable of exciting an easy and spontaneous joy and delight. To aid them in achieving the splendor of beauty, all the arts make use of the device of contrast. Just as in pure reasoning the mind is more impressed by the presentation of the opposite, so it is with all the faculties involved in the appreciation of beauty. They function with greater facility when they can compare one thing with another and thus they produce aesthetic pleasure with greater ease and force because they enable the mind to view the object in its proper perspective so as to give a greater amount of enjoyment.

From ancient times beauty has been the subject of great controversy, and almost every philosopher and artist has tried his hand at explaining it. Few have been satisfied with the attempts. The reason for this is that the aesthetic pleasure which beauty gives is ultimately a psychological experience which cannot be completely analyzed, or at least never has been completely analyzed. One of the best attempts at such a psychological analysis is the essay *On the Sublime and Beautiful* by Edmund Burke. He comes to grips with the problem in the field of man's emotions, which is precisely the point of difficulty, since these reactions are so diverse on account of individual and racial temperament and educational and cultural environment. There are such great differences of opinion about what constitutes the beautiful that men have despaired of solving the problem. This is expressed in the old adage, *De gustibus non est disputandum.*

While we admit that the matter may never be completely settled to the satisfaction even of the majority, nevertheless a discussion of the problem leads to a better understanding and a deeper appreciation of the beautiful itself and of the aesthetic pleasure which it causes in us.

SUMMARY OF CHAPTER XI

1 **Nature of truth.** The fundamental notion of truth is true knowledge, which consists in true judgments—that is, when the mind agrees with reality. There is also truth in things when they agree with the mind. Truth in general is the conformity between intellect and thing.

2 **Kinds of truth.** Ontological truth is the conformity of a thing to the intellect. Logical truth is the conformity of the intellect to the thing. Moral truth is the conformity of speech to thought.

3 **Foundation of truth.** Ontological truth must have its ultimate foundation in the intellect of that being whose essence is the ultimate foundation of all reality. Hence the ultimate foundation of all truth consists in the essential conformity of all things with the divine mind.

4 **Convertibility of being and truth.** All being is ontologically true because it is in conformity with the divine mind. If truth is an attribute of being, truth must be something and not nothing; therefore whatever is true is a being.

5 **Nature of falsity.** In the absolute sense there is no ontological falsity because all being is ontologically true. Relatively—with regard to the human mind—things may be said to be ontologically false when false judgments are made concerning them.

6 **Properties of truth.** Truth is primarily an attribute of the mind of God and is only secondarily and analogically applied to things. Truth is said to be eternal and immutable because it is an attribute of God's knowledge, which is eternal and immutable.

7 **Pragmatism.** Pragmatism holds the relativity of all truth, that what is true today may be false tomorrow. Expediency thus becomes the measure of truth. Such a doctrine evidently denies the existence of a supreme intelligence.

8 **Truth of the contingent future.** Contingently future events are those which depend upon the decision of a free will. Have such events any present truth? The answer is yes. Their truth can now be expressed in two contradictory statements, one of which will be true in the future and the other of which will be false. If it has truth, it is known to God from eternity. The futurible, as it is called, is more of an object of knowledge than is the mere possible; *a fortiori,* therefore, it must be known if the possible is known.

9 **Nature of goodness.** Goodness is that which is suitable to a natural appetency or desire. Whatever satisfies its nature is good for a thing. There are three kinds of good. Ontological good consists in the being or reality of the thing itself insofar as it represents the being of God. Physical good is that which perfects the nature of a being. Moral good is a

quality of actions by which they are conformable to their proper standard.

10 **Convertibility of being and goodness.** Every being is good because every being has a nature suitable to itself, which is a perfection, and, therefore, desirable and good. Whatever is good is a being since the good cannot be nothing but must be some suitable thing. Goodness as a transcendental attribute of being applies to both ontological and physical good because both are present in every being as an act or perfection of some kind.

11 **Nature and theories of evil.** Evil is not a positive reality; it is a privation of some good and hence a privative non-being. There are as many kinds of evil as there are good. Pessimism is a false doctrine because it considers evil as a positive being. Zoroastrianism and Manichaeism are absurd teachings which maintain the existence of two supreme principles, one of good and one of evil.

12 **Subjective elements in beauty.** St. Thomas' definition of beauty is, "Those things are beautiful which please when seen." Beauty gives aesthetic pleasure which is not selfish but disinterested. The pleasure is mainly intellectual but must arise in the senses through an imaginative appeal. The appeal is ultimately to the intellect and not the will, although desire will accompany the pleasure in some way because of the goodness in the object.

13 **Objective elements in beauty.** Unity, truth, and goodness are to be found in the beautiful, although the beautiful is not a transcendental and is not identical with any of them. St. Thomas enumerates three particular objective requirements of the beautiful: integrity or completeness, proportion or balance, and clarity or splendor. Aesthetic pleasure is ultimately a psychological experience incapable of complete analysis.

CHAPTER XII

THE CATEGORIES OF ARISTOTLE

IT is the purpose of this chapter to try to find some arrangement or classification into which we can place reality in general so as to examine each kind in more detail. We have already discussed several classes into which being can be divided; we will now investigate other divisions which will include all real being and by which we can distinguish the various kinds one from another. Such a system is found in the categories of Aristotle, which are, as we shall see, a practical arrangement for examining the relationships between various kinds of reality. In this division we find another example of the genius for common sense so characteristic of Aristotle. Before his time there had been little attempt to classify being in any orderly arrangement, and the classifications that had been made were inadequate. It was the common sense of the Stagirite that enabled him to see the desirability and usefulness of the division of reality into classes, just as any reasonable person would find a place for everything and try to keep things in their proper place.

Definition of the term "category"

The term *category* in its present sense comes down to us from the time of Aristotle. The Greek word *kategoria* meant an accusation or charge and was used in the law courts for the charge against the defendant in a suit. Just as the law courts render their judgments in cases that have been brought before them, so the mind makes its judgments or decisions about reality. Aristotle, therefore, transferred the word from a legal use to a logical use in the sense of attributing one thing to another as we do in predicating a quality of a subject. The primary meaning of category as the word is used in philosophy, therefore, is one of the supreme classes of predicates as found in our judgments and propositions.

The categories in this sense belong to the science of logic and have been explained there. But since predicates represent ideas, and since ideas represent things in Aristotelian philosophy, the word also had an ontological sense—it also included the things which the ideas represented. In this meaning the categories were the supreme classes of real beings, and in this sense the explanation of them belongs to ontology. The term *kategoria* was translated into Latin by the word *praedicamentum*. Both words have been anglicized, and in fact have become part of almost all European languages. The use of the term *predicament* to mean *a difficult situation* is common in English, and its original signification of a class to which a thing belongs and out of which it can scarcely be moved is quite obvious in the derived usage.

The purpose of the categories

There is no science of the individual as such. For this reason classification is a necessary part of any scientific system. The number of particular items of knowledge that could be predicated of an individual is negatively infinite, and also changes from moment to moment. It would be a hopeless task to try to enumerate everything that could be said about a thing during every moment of its existence, and a task that would produce only chaos and confusion rather than serviceable information. The purpose of the categories is to reduce this chaotic mass to order and system. The categories arrange all reality into a few general classes, thus assisting the mind in the task of interpreting the manifold of experience.

We have already discussed the division of being into substance and accident. In a further examination of this division Aristotle found five important divisions of the idea of accident: quantity, quality, relation, action, and passion. For the sake of completeness he added four others which resemble the first group, at least to some extent. He then had the complete list of substance and nine accidents as a workable division of all reality. His division was neither too small nor too large, and included every important mode or kind of being, so that it was reasonably complete. Aristotle was enabled to enumerate these classes simply by asking himself what were the fundamental questions which could be asked about any reality; in answering those questions he arrived at the categories. How these categories were imitated and borrowed from even in Roman times is shown by the so-called common places or *loci communes* of Tertullian and the other grammarians of antiquity: *quis, quid, ubi, per quos, quoties, cur, quommodo, quando;* that is, *who, what, where, by whose means, how often, why, how,* and *when.* The similarity between the lists is apparent, as it is also in the headings given for the description of a person: *forma, figura, locus, tempus, stirps, partia, nomen,* which would be translated *shape, height, place, time, ancestry, country, name.*

The categories of Aristotle

Aristotle distinguished ten categories: substance and the nine accidents of quantity, quality, relation, action, passion, where or place, when or time, posture, and habitus or external condition. We find them enumerated in the fourth chapter of the *Organon* as follows:

> Of things simple in their nature, each signifies either substance or quantity or quality or relation or where or when or position (posture) or possession (habitus) or action or passion. But substance is to speak generally, as man, horse; quantity, as two or three cubits; quality, as white; relation, as greater; where, as in the forum; when, as yesterday; position, as he sits; possession, as he is shod; action, as he cuts; passion, as he burns.

A brief explanation of some of these categories may be helpful. A substance is a being which exists in itself. It is opposed to an accident *(ens in alio),* which inheres in a substance. The other nine categories are accidents, beings which inhere in another. *Quantity* is an attribute of the material element in a being—its extension, number, weight, or size. Aristotle's horse, for example, is three cubits high and weighs two thousand pounds. *Quality* is an attribute of the form in a being: the man is white, the horse is a roan. *Relation* consists in a reference of one thing to another, a comparison of one thing with another: the horse is heavier than the man. *Where* is position in space: the horse is in the forum. *When* is situation in time: yesterday morning. *Position* or *posture* refers to attitude, the disposition of the parts of a being: the man sits, the horse is upright. *Possession* or *habitus* is the state or condition of a being with reference to external things: the horse is shod, the man is fully accoutered. *Action* is the production of an effect: the man is riding, the horse is galloping. *Passion* is the reception of the action in another: the horse is being ridden, the boxer is being beaten by his opponent.

Along with all other scholastic writers St. Thomas adopts the categories of Aristotle in their entirety. He explains them in great detail in his commentary on the *Metaphysics*. A diagram including all the categories could readily be built up from the explanation of St. Thomas.

Some philosophers in modern times have expressed criticism of the categories of Aristotle, claiming that they are not mutually exclusive but that there is considerable overlapping in the divisions. They say, for instance, that action and passion are only two phases of one and the same thing: that viewed from the standpoint of the agent, it is action; that viewed from the standpoint of the recipient, it is reaction or passion. This is indeed true, but the agent and the recipient are usually two different entities, and surely action and passion are not the same thing in themselves. Cause and effect are in fact really distinct, in spite of the fact that they are by nature closely connected. The categories of time, place, and posture also are really subordinate categories to those of quantity and relation. There is, however, at least a logical distinction with a foundation in reality between them, and this is a sufficient reason for distinguishing them as categories. The categories were intended primarily as classes of universal concepts; therefore if they differ in concept, they are at least logically distinct categories. The differences among them are founded in reality, however, and this makes them different ontological divisions also. We must also remember that Aristotle's purpose was essentially practical, and that these are all theoretical objections. He would have been justified in making a different category if one was too extensive or if the matter could be treated more advantageously by a new division, so long as there was some slight difference in reality or in thought.

Placement in a category

All finite being can be placed in the categories in one way or another. Scholastic philosophers enumerate three ways in which a being can be placed in a category: directly, indirectly or obliquely, and reductively or by reason of some connection with a being which belongs in that category directly or indirectly. God of course is not included in any category. He is indeed a substance, but is not in the category of substance because that idea or any other idea can be predicated of God and creatures only analogously and not univocally. Only finite being is placed in the categories: the infinite is outside of and above them.

The simplest way that a being may be placed in a category is of course directly. Thus man, dog, animal, book, and tree all fall directly under the category of substance. If a being does not fall directly into a category, it may be placed in one either indirectly or reductively. For instance, the differences which exist between genera and species come indirectly into the category of substance because the genera and species themselves belong in this category directly. Such are the concepts of rationality, spirituality, sentiency, and the like. Parts of things, whether integral or substantial; beings with only an artificial unity; and even logical beings or nothings are brought reductively under their corresponding categories. Thus arms and legs, family, army, nation, belong to the category of substance; blindness, ignorance, the intensity of heat, and the power of light belong under quality; curve and triangularity are placed under quantity.

As is apparent from what has already been said, accidents may be related to their subjects in different ways. Three of them are in the subject, although one of these in a very different manner from the other two, as will become clear later on; two are only partially in the subject; and four are entirely outside the subject. It is rather obvious, then, that the definition of accident, that which inheres in a subject, applies to these entities in a somewhat different manner. The concept of accident applies to some of them in an analogical sense only. Accident cannot be predicated univocally of quantity and time, for example. One confers a real perfection upon the substance, and the other confers only an external relation. Hence the concept of accident is not a true genus, since its modes are not true species but only practical divisions of the general concept.

These theoretical difficulties do not in the least affect the practical usefulness of the Aristotelian classification. In spite of them it has become an integral part of the language and mode of thought of Western culture. There have been in modern times some attempts to supplant the categories of Aristotle, but without much success. The best known of such efforts is the categories of Kant, which we shall now discuss.

The Kantian categories

Immanuel Kant (1724-1804), a German philosopher, did much to popularize idealism and subjectivism in modern times. The popularity of his doctrines in all branches of philosophy, and especially in epistemology, is one of the major reasons why it is important to give space to a statement of his position and a refutation of his teachings. Kant's intentions were undoubtedly good, and he had great intellectual gifts. He had read very little in the field of philosophy, however, and that little was mostly in secondary sources. His background was further limited because he had never traveled beyond Germany and not much within it. In addition, he was seldom willing to lend an open ear and an open mind to the advice and opinions of others. Moreover, he was a child of a rationalistic age and was much influenced by the thought of the French Revolution, and especially by Jean Jacques Rousseau. Chronologically, the first phase of his thought was rationalistic; empiricism and skepticism were secondary phases.

Kant's philosophy was an attempt to answer the phenomenalism and skepticism of Locke and Hume, which were very popular throughout Europe at that time. One of his fundamental principles is the distinction between *things-in-themselves (dingen-an-sich* or *noumena)* and the *phenomena* or *appearances* of things. The noumena are real things independent of our thinking, but the mind is of its nature incapable of ever knowing anything about them. The noumena are the existing causes of our sensible knowledge, and the result of the action of the senses is the production of sense intuitions or phenomena. These phenomena are the objects of our knowledge but they do not represent reality; they are a subjective response to reality. According to Kant, in order to have this subjective experience at all, there must exist in the mind the *a-priori* forms of space and time; without these subjective forms no sense knowledge would be possible at all.

For Kant the word *transcendental* had an entirely different meaning than it has for the scholastic philosopher. He used it to mean a condition which must be in the mind in order for cognition to take place. The first of these conditions or transcendentals are the *a-priori* forms of space and time, which are in the senses and which make possible the cognition of external space and internal states (time).

Kant's so-called categories are such transcendental conditions for intellectual knowledge. They are subjective forms or modes into which the data of sense experience are fitted, much as a form for concrete would give it a particular shape. Our cognition, according to Kant, arises

KANTIAN CATEGORIES AND JUDGMENTS

Categories	*Judgments*	*Examples*
Quantity:	Quantity:	
1. Unity	1. Singular	This S is P
2. Plurality	2. Particular	Some S is P
3. Totality	3. Universal	All S is P
Quality:	Quality:	
4. Affirmation	4. Affirmative	S is P
5. Negation	5. Negative	S is not P
6. Limitation	6. Infinite	S is non-P
Relation:	Relation:	
7. Substantiality	7. Categorical	S is P
8. Causality	8. Hypothetical	If A is B, S is P
9. Reciprocity	9. Disjunctive	S is either P or Q
Modality:	Modality:	
10. Possibility	10. Problematic	S may be P
11. Existence	11. Assertoric	S is P
12. Necessity	12. Apodictic	S must be P

from the union of these forms with the phenomena of sense experience. The forms are part of the furniture of the mind and are applied to the phenomena according to the law of the mind's nature so as to give us the knowledge we have. Such knowledge obviously would not consist in a representation of things but in a representation of the mind's own subjective states, and it would reveal nothing whatever about the noumena or things-in-themselves.

Kant lists twelve categories and twelve corresponding classes of judgments. The categories include such subjective forms as totality, substantiality, causality, existence, necessity, and the like. According to Kant's explanation of these categories in the *Critique of Pure Reason,* all the ideas listed under the categories are pure mental constructs, entirely independent of experience and pre-existing as modes of thought antecedent to all knowledge derived from experience. They are means of reducing to order the purely subjective operations of the mind. Their purpose is to unify the manifold of sense experience and to impose on it, as it were, the forms of necessity and universality. They tell us nothing of the reality which exists independently of the mind. Hence they bear no resemblance to the Aristotelian categories, which are classes of direct universal ideas and modes of real being. Kant's categories, on the contrary, are kinds of mental judgment forms and modes of logical relations.

A great many modern philosophers have followed Kant's interpretation of reality and as a result have developed phenomenalistic and subjectivistic philosophies. Many scientists have been influenced by these philosophies, and maintain that we can know only the appearances of things and that the noumenal world is entirely beyond our knowledge. They also deny all objective validity to such ideas as substance, accident, cause, and the like. Thus from its small beginnings in the philosophy of Immanuel Kant has developed one of the most common and most serious errors in modern thought.

SUMMARY OF CHAPTER XII

1 **Nature of the categories.** The categories or predicaments are the supreme kinds of direct universal ideas, and therefore are modes of real being. As a supreme class of ideas or predicates they have a logical meaning and as modes of real being they are used in an ontological sense.

2 **Purpose of the categories.** The purpose of the categories is to reduce to order and system—to classify—all the different kinds of real being.

3 **Placement of being in the categories.** The categories are ten in number, including substance and nine classes of accidents: substance, quantity, quality, relation, action, passion, place, time, posture, and habitus. The term *accident* does not apply to all nine accidents in exactly the same sense; it is used analogously.

All reality may be placed in these classes in one of three ways—directly, indirectly, or reductively. If a being does not belong in a category directly, it can be said to do so either indirectly or reductively; that is, by reason of some connection or relation to a being which comes directly under that particular category.

4 **The Kantian categories.** Kant's categories are classes of mental judgment forms and modes of logical relations and not classes of real being like the categories of Aristotle. They are innate mental forms which can give us no knowledge of the noumena or reality but only of our own subjective states or phenomena. Kant's subjectivistic philosophy, with all its flaws and errors, has exercised a profound influence on modern thought.

CHAPTER XIII

SUBSTANCE AND ACCIDENT

SUBSTANCE is obviously the first and most important of the categories; it is also the one concerning which there has been the most controversy. A substance is a being whose nature it is to exist in itself and not in another as in a subject. An accident, on the other hand, is a being whose nature it is to exist in another as in a subject of inhesion. From the very definitions it is obvious that the one is dependent on the other and that, therefore, being is predicated of them not univocally but analogously.

From the standpoint of experience we come first to the knowledge of accidents, such as size, shape, weight, and color. Then we observe that many of these things are in a state of constant flux, and yet that there is something which can be said to be relatively permanent amidst all these changes. Thus we conclude to the existence of substance, the underlying subject of these accidental changes. Our senses lead us to the knowledge of the modifications which we call accidents. Our reason tells us that there must be a sort of being on which these qualities depend and which itself is independent of another being as a subject of inhesion; in other words, a being which stands by itself, a being *per se,* a substance. It should be noticed that we do not say that the substance is independent in every way, but only in the sense that it does not need a subject of inhesion. A being *per se* is obviously not necessarily also a being *a se;* that is, entirely independent in its being. Naturally, however, or from the standpoint of being itself, the substance is first and the accident secondary because the accident is only a modification of the substance and presupposes the existence of the substance, since its own existence is a dependent one.

Substance, then, can be considered from two viewpoints: as a thing in general in itself or as a support for accidents. The primary concept is as a thing in itself; to consider it as a support for accidents is a secondary concept. It must be a thing in itself before it can be a support for others. Even if a substance had no accidents at all, it would still have its own entity and would be a true substance. This is in fact the case with God, who has and could have no accidents and is nonetheless the first substance, being *per se* and *a se,* possessing in His infinite essence all the perfections which accidents could confer upon Him. Accidents presuppose the concept of substance, but substance does not necessarily include the concept of accident.

An accident always presupposes a subject of which it is a determination, and this subject of inhesion is ultimately a substance. It is not necessary that every accident inhere immediately in a substance; it may inhere in another accident. Shape, for instance, inheres directly in quantity, and quantity directly modifies the substance. The substance is in potency to all kinds of accidental perfections, and the accidents are the realization or actualization of those potencies. Thus all our acts of thinking, willing, and sense perception are accidents which perfect the faculty involved and, therefore, the substantial ego which supports them all.

Kinds of substance

There are a number of divisions of substance, only one of which, the division into primary substance and secondary substance, is important to our present purpose. The others will be given only brief attention, since they are the subject matter of other branches of philosophy.

Plato was the first philosopher to make a serious attempt to explain the universality and necessity of our ideas. Our knowledge, he reasoned, is universal and necessary, and if it is a true representation of reality, then the reality must itself likewise be universal and necessary. But Plato saw no evidence of any such qualities of universality and necessity in the physical world as he knew it: all things were individual and in a constant process of change. He could see no reason, therefore, for the universality of our ideas and knowledge in the things of this world. Since the concept or idea in our mind represented the essence of things objectively, he was led to the conclusion that the essence or ideas, being the only realities which are universal and necessary, must exist physically in a separate world of their own, eternal and unchangeable. They would then be universal and necessary, and exemplars according to which the physical things of this world would be fashioned and of which our ideas are representations. The individual physical things of this world would be copies of the universal physical things of that other world, which according to Plato were still *ideas,* and of which our subjective ideas were images. These ideas were the primary substance, and the individual substances of this world were secondary substances.

Aristotle maintained that there was no necessity for the existence of a separate world of ideas actually existing as universal physical things. He founded his doctrine on the principle explained in psychology: *Nihil est in intellectu quod non prius fuerit aliquo modo in sensu—There is nothing in the intellect which was not previously in some way in the senses.* We form universal ideas from a consideration of the individual physical things around us. By a process of abstraction the mind, ignoring the individuating differences between things, forms an idea of their essence which is common to all the individuals of a class. In the Aristotelian doctrine, therefore, the primary substance is the actually existing individual thing; the secondary substance is the universal idea that the mind forms of the essence of that being and which it has in common with other beings.

As has already been pointed out in a previous chapter, Plato was not wholly wrong in attributing reality to the idea or essence. Ideas and essences are possible beings and as such have reality, metaphysical reality, metaphysical being, although they do not have physical or actually existing being as Plato thought. The reality of the potential in this sense is the foundation of the doctrine of potency and act and hence of the whole Aristotelian system.

Substance may also be divided into simple and composite substance. A simple substance is one which does not consist of substantial parts, such as the human soul. A composite substance is one which does consist of substantial parts, such as man, who is composed of soul and body.

Substances are either complete or incomplete. A complete substance is one which of itself is not ordained to form a union with a substantial coprinciple, such as a man or an angel. A substance is incomplete when it is ordained to be united with a substantial coprinciple, as are the body and soul of man.

Empiricism and substance

The existence of substance has been denied, especially in modern times, by such men as Hume, John Stuart Mill, William James, and in general by empiricists, sensists, materialists, phenomenalists, and pragmatists—a formidable array including practically all philosophers outside the Aristotelian school. Kant, too, denied the objective validity of the idea of substance, and the idealistic monism of Hegel is necessarily built on the premise that there is only one substance, the infinite. Hume, to take an example from the sensist school, built his theory on the contention that our knowledge of phenomena was the only valid knowledge. If there is anything more than phenomena, it is unknown and unknowable because there is no such thing as intellectual knowledge in the Aristotelian sense. The idea of substance has no objective validity; it is but a figment of the mind, by which Hume means a sense faculty.

> The idea of substance must therefore be derived from an impression of reflection, if it really exist. But the impressions of reflection resolve themselves into our passions and emotions, none of which can possibly represent a substance. We have therefore no idea of substance distinct from that of a collection of particular qualities, nor have we any other meaning when we either talk or reason concerning it.[1]

This is a typical expression of sensist doctrine. The senses are the only means of knowledge man has, and he can therefore know only phenomena. In the passage quoted, Hume implicitly denies that there is an intellect or intellectual knowledge. There are only the senses and the passions and emotions. Such a doctrine leads to universal skepticism, for without the action of the intellect to interpret sense experience, true knowledge is impossible.

The existence of substance

The validity of the idea of substance as it is understood in Aristotelian philosophy is based on very simple and evident reasoning which has never been refuted by its strongest opponents. The argument is usually proposed in the following manner: If anything exists, then substance must exist. But actual beings exist. Therefore substance must exist. The minor must be admitted in order to avoid universal skepticism. The major is proved thus: If anything exists, it must exist either in itself or in

[1] David Hume, *Treatise on Human Nature,* Pt. 1, Sec. 6.

another. (This is a complete division by dichotomy and is based on the principle of contradiction—everything must be either in itself or not in itself; that is, in another.) If it exists in itself, it corresponds to the definition of substance, and therefore substance exists. If it exists in another as in a subject, then we must inquire into the existence of this other. Does it exist in itself or again in another? If in itself, then we have a substance. If in another, then we must again inquire into the nature of this other. Since an infinite series is impossible—a contradiction in terms—we must eventually come to something which exists in itself, a substance and a subject of inhesion for beings which are unable to inhere in themselves.

The existence of substance may also be proved by a second argument, the argument from internal experience. Consciousness makes us aware of all our actions of sensing, thinking, and willing as real, accidental modifications of the ego or self which has these acts. We are never aware of these acts as if they existed in a detached state, but of ourselves as having these acts, of the ego as having these modifications. We cannot truly express the facts of internal experience without using the personal pronoun to express the self: I think, I will, I feel. We thereby connect the activity with the subject of the activity, the substance which produces the acts with the acts which are produced by it. From the facts of consciousness, therefore, it follows that the subject modified as well as the modification is reported to us by our internal experience, and consequently the idea of substance must represent something that belongs to reality; that is, the idea of substance has objective validity.

The conclusion that the existence of substance—of something existing in itself—must be admitted to explain the facts of experience is so unavoidable that even those who are unwilling to admit the existence of substance finally arrive at a position that would make substances out of accidents. William James, for instance, is satisfied that he has explained away substance when he says that the present thought is the thinker, but he has really succeeded only in making a substance of the individual thought.

Nature and kinds of accidents

Since accidents are beings which can exist only in another, Aristotle held that they were beings only in a qualified sense. Scholastic philosophers refer to them as *entia secundum quid,* being not strictly but in a derived sense. The substance is *ens, being;* the accident is *ens entis,* the *being of a being*. The accident is a modification of the subject; its reality is in the subject as a modification. By reason of the inherence of the accident, the substance has a new perfection, a new actuality. This of course is not a denial of the reality of accidents. They have reality, but it is a reality in the subject, a reality once potential in that subject but now reduced to act by the accident. Substance is being in the full and independent sense. An accident has being in a derived and dependent sense; it has being only analogously according to an analogy of intrinsic attribution. In order to understand accidents correctly we must keep constantly in mind this fact, that whatever reality an accident may have, that reality is not something that exists independently in itself, but something that must exist in another, the substance.

A question also arises concerning the nature of the distinction between substance and accident. Is it real or only mental? The answer is that there is a real distinction in many cases. The being of the accident is the being of the substance, but not in such a way that its being *constitutes* the substance. We know from both internal and external experience that it is possible for all that is substantial in a thing to remain when one accident is removed and replaced by another. The substance is changed, of course, but the change is only an accidental change and not a substantial one. Now, if two realities—in this case substance and accident—are separate in the sense that one remains in existence when the other has ceased to exist, there is a real distinction between them by the test of separability. This is the universal scholastic doctrine.

Accidents may be looked at in different ways and placed in different classes according to the aspect being considered. For example, accidents may be either relative or absolute. (By a relation is meant the reference which one thing has to another. Thus there must be two terms in every relation.) When we speak of an accident as being *relative* we mean that it has being in a subject because of its reference to another being, called the term of the relation. An *absolute* accident is one that confers a real perfection upon its subject. Quantity is an absolute accident. It supposes quantitative parts outside of parts, and these parts are a real perfection for a thing. Qualities are also absolute accidents. The power of nutrition in plants, the faculty of sensation in animals, the faculties of intellect and will in man, are all qualities and all constitute real perfections for their subjects. All actions reduce the faculty from potency to act and therefore confer a perfection upon the subject which is the ultimate cause of them.

A *modal* accident is a disposition or determination of a being which does not confer any new entity upon the substance. These modes are something real, but their reality is entirely inseparable from the subject in which they inhere. Such are shape, rest or motion, time, place, and posture.

Intrinsic accidents are those which affect the being of a subject; they are internal perfections of the being. Quantity and quality are intrinsic accidents. *Extrinsic* accidents do not affect the being of the subject but modify it indirectly and externally. Such are time, place, posture, and habitus. The difference between intrinsic and extrinsic accidents is a clear indication of why the term *accident* must be predicated analogously of these different kinds of accident.

The diagram on page 176 may serve to clarify these various divisions of accidents.

Proof of the existence of absolute accidents

The real distinction between substance and accident was denied by René Descartes, who contended that thought is the essence of spiritual substance and extension the essence of material substance; hence that there are no such things as absolute accidents, but all accidents are relative, consisting only in differences of position or the reference of one substance to another. The following three proofs are offered in refutation of the Cartesian position and in support of the doctrine of the real distinction between substance and accident and of the existence of absolute accidents.

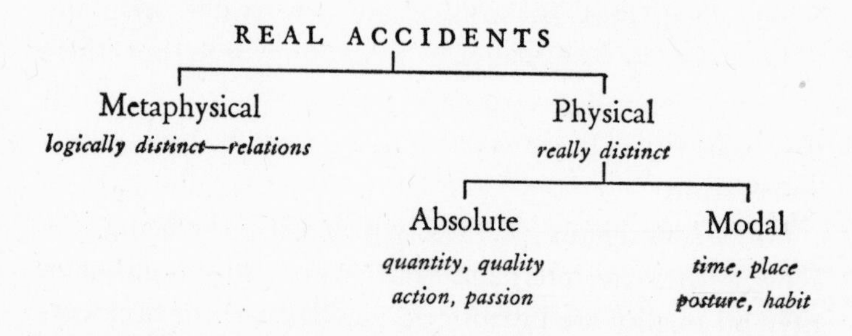

The first proof is from internal experience. Our consciousness testifies to the vegetative, sensitive, and rational acts of our complex being and recognizes them as modifications of the substantial self or ego. To deny this testimony of consciousness is to fall into universal skepticism. We perceive, then, two types of reality: the one which does not exist in itself, which is present for a time and then disappears; and the other which does stand by itself, furnishes support for these modifications, and persists in being after their disappearance. The first reality is an accident which truly confers a new perfection on the substance which supports it in being. The second reality is a substance which retains its essential identity and remains permanent amid these mutations. These mutations and qualities, therefore, are real beings, really distinct from their substance.

Just as we may reason to the truth about our own internal acts of sensation, thinking, and willing, so we may reason to the same conclusion about other beings. We see the accidents of quantity, quality, and so forth in any particular being constantly changing, while at the same time there persists in the subject of these changes an essential substrate. The modifications themselves are without doubt real, and the test of separability proves them to be really distinct from their substances. A real being which comes and goes and a real being which persists during these changes cannot possibly be the same thing.

Then, too, our actions produce results. Thinking produces knowledge, and decisions of the will result in a virtuous or vicious state of soul. If knowledge and virtue are not realities distinct from the reality of the soul, then the soul could never change its state from ignorance to knowledge or from vice to virtue. But it is contrary to all our experience to say that the soul does not really change when it advances from ignorance to knowledge or from vice to virtue. Knowledge and virtue, then, are real perfections and are really distinct from the substance of the soul. The effort we make to acquire them ought of itself to convince us that the soul cannot be the same before and after their acquisition.

SUMMARY OF CHAPTER XIII

1 **Substance and accident.** A substance is a being whose nature it is to exist in itself. An accident is a being whose nature it is to exist in another as in a subject of inhesion. Our senses report modifications which we call accidents;

our reason tells us that there must be a subject to support them. The primary concept of substance is as a thing in itself; the secondary concept is as a subject for accidents. Substance does not necessarily include the concept of accidents; there may be substance without accidents.

2 **Kinds of substance.** According to Aristotle the primary substance is the individually existing thing; the universal idea formed from it is the secondary substance. The doctrine of Plato was the reversal of this. He postulated a physical world in which ideas existed unchangeable and eternal. It is true that ideas or essences have unchangeable and eternal reality, but it is a metaphysical reality rather than a physical reality. Substance is also simple or composite, complete or incomplete.

3 **Empiricism and substance.** Empiricists and phenomenalists deny the existence of substance and hold that we have only sense knowledge and that the senses can know only phenomena or the appearance of things. This is a denial of reason as a source of knowledge and amounts to universal skepticism.

4 **The existence of substance.** Actual beings exist. They must exist either in themselves or in another. If they exist in themselves, they are substances. If they exist in another, we must inquire of this other, "Does it exist in itself or in another?" Unless we wish to postulate an infinite series, we must finally rest in a being which exists in itself. An infinite series actually existing is a contradiction.

A second argument is taken from internal experience. Consciousness reports our internal states as modifications of the substantial ego. It reports the self as subject and the states of consciousness as modifications of the self in the same datum of experience. The self as subject must then be a substance.

5 **Nature and kinds of accidents.** The accident is being *secundum quid,* not being in itself *(simpliciter),* but a being of a being *(ens entis).* It has its reality in the subject. Some accidents are really distinct from substance. A relative accident (relation) is the reference of one thing to another. An absolute accident is one that confers a real perfection upon the substance. Quantity and quality are such absolute accidents. A modal accident is a kind of determination of a being which does not confer any reality upon the subject. It is not really distinct from the being of its substance. Intrinsic accidents are internal perfections of the substance; extrinsic accidents are those which affect the being externally.

6 **Proof of absolute accidents.** Descartes denied the existence of absolute accidents. Their existence can be proved particularly from internal experience. In all our conscious acts we are aware of two types of reality, one which comes and goes, the other which persists in being amid these changes. But a real being which persists and one which remains for a time and then disappears cannot be one and the same thing. Therefore the self and its thoughts and desires are two different things.

CHAPTER XIV

QUALITY AND RELATION

ONTOLOGY does not treat of all the categories. The human soul, an immaterial substance, is studied in psychology. Quantity and categories closely related to quantity, such as time, place, posture, and habitus, belong to cosmology, which treats of material being. The general nature of the remaining accidents—quality, relation, action, and passion—will be treated in the following chapters.

In a wide sense the term quality may mean any sort of modification. All specific differences are spoken of as qualities even though they are part of the essence of the being. For instance, rationality is often called a quality of man. So too almost any kind of accident, even quantity, is called a quality of the substance. When, however, quality is taken in its strict sense as a category distinct from all others, it is defined by Aristotle as "that by virtue of which things are said to be such and such."[1] This defini-

[1] *Organon, Categoriae,* cap. 8, b. 25.

tion still does not distinguish quality from quantity or relation with any degree of clarity. Later philosophers define quality as an *absolute accident completing and determining a substance in its being and in its operations.* By remembering that quality is an accident following the form and not the matter and by adding some examples to this descriptive definition, quality may be fairly well distinguished from the other categories.

Four distinct types of quality are generally enumerated: habit and disposition; natural capacity and incapacity; affective qualities and affections; form and figure. All these qualities may be reduced to two main groups: entitative qualities which modify the substance in its being, and operative qualities which modify it in its operations. This classification is not perfect, however, and there is some overlapping. Thus, the same quality can be placed in different classes, depending upon the viewpoint; heat, for example, may be regarded either as a natural operative power of a substance or as a sensible quality produced in that substance by another power.

Habit and disposition

A habit is usually defined as *a quality, stable and difficult to remove, disposing a thing well or ill in its being or in its operations.* Habit implies the more or less permanent possession of a facility in the performance of the actions which belong to the faculty which possesses it. Habits which are perfections of the being are beauty, knowledge, and virtue. Bad habits would be ugliness, ignorance, and vice.

If a quality is not permanent but relatively transient in nature, it is called a disposition rather than a habit; qualities that dispose the being to evil rather than to good are called indispositions. An example of a disposition would be a temporary feeling of well-being produced by a good which could not be lasting, such as the enjoyment of a beautiful object. Examples of an indisposition would be a headache or an upset stomach. If a disposition ceases to be a relatively transient thing and becomes permanent, it would then be called a habit.

A habit may affect the being either in its nature or in its operations. Habits which affect operations are called operative habits. Operative habits are acquired by the repetition of acts. Each repetition strengthens the habit and makes it easier to perform the act the next time the occasion arises. In time a habit can become almost automatic and without any conscious effort. Examples of the exercise of operative habits would be playing the piano or any other musical instrument, playing a game that requires a certain skill, or writing shorthand. We can appreciate the usefulness of operative habits when we recall our first attempts to swim and the final facility we attained after months of practice.

Not all the faculties of a being can be improved by habit, but only those which of their nature are indifferent to a variety of actions and can thus be determined to a particular one. The physical forces of nature are not the subject of habits, nor are vegetative and sensitive processes, since they act with physical necessity. Strictly speaking, only beings which are free in their activities can be the subjects of habit.

The intellect and will of man, therefore, are the primary subjects of habits. Knowledge is an intellectual habit; virtue is a moral habit. Since, however, all of man's free actions are subject to the control of the will, the faculties which produce them are also said to have habits. Although brute animals are not the subjects of habits in the strict sense, since they lack free will, we speak of them as having habits because in many things they are not determined by nature and may be trained or taught to do things in one way rather than another.

Some habits are natural in the sense that nature furnishes them along with the faculty of which they are habits. Thus scholastic philosophy speaks of the *habitus principiorum,* the habit of principles, as present in the mind from its beginning. The meaning is that the mind has a natural facility to form such principles of thought as the principles of contradiction, excluded middle, and sufficient reason, and the fundamental moral principles.

Most habits, however, are acquired by the repetition of acts and may be increased to a considerable degree of perfection. They may also be diminished or entirely lost by lack of practice in the acts which form them. Usually it is much easier to form habits than it is to break them. This is especially true of evil habits.

An understanding of the nature of habit is very important for the science of ethics, since habit profoundly affects the morality of acts. In ontology, however, we are simply interested in the general nature of habit as modifying a faculty by making it more or less perfect. Even though the habit were an evil one, the facility acquired in performing the act would be a physical perfection in the ontological sense. A habit does not consist in the mere repetition of the act. The repetition must leave behind it some result of the action in the faculty itself, a facility for performing the act that is strengthened by each repetition. This result, the modification of the faculty, is the reality of the habit. It is a different reality than the faculty because it is in addition to it. We see, then, that evil habits are evil only in the sense that they lead more readily to evil acts. In themselves, as things added to the faculty, they are metaphysical and physical goods, just as are the faculties which they modify.

Other kinds of qualities

Natural capacities or faculties are another important type of quality. Natural capacities are distinguished from habits by the fact that the capacities or faculties are proximate accidental principles of operation in a being, the substance itself of course being the ultimate principle of operation. The faculty is the subject of the habit and could operate without the habit, which merely facilitates the action. The faculty is the source of activity, while the habit is only a modifier of that source. The natural capacity or faculty as the immediate principle of operation makes the being fully prepared to act, even though the action may take place only intermittently. For example, the intellect and will are always capable of action, but we are not always thinking or willing. By an incapacity, as opposed to a capacity, Aristotle did not mean the total absence of a faculty, but rather that it was in an unfit condition for operation. Thus the mind of man may be affected by idiocy or insanity, or his will may be affected by sleep or drugs.

There are also qualities which produce or result from some sensible alteration. Such a quality is called an affective quality if it is relatively permanent; if it is temporary in character, it is called an affection. The ruddiness of one's complexion and the fragrance of a rose would be affective qualities. A blush or a blanching of the skin would be an affection. The sweetness of an apple would be an affective quality which could cause the perception of sweetness in the person who ate it; the effect, the perception, would be an affection. Temperament would also be an affective quality.[2]

Form or figure is the quality in a body that results from the arrangement of its quantitative parts. The shape of a geometrical quantity is usually called figure, while the shape of a natural body is called form. A triangle, a circle, or a square is a figure, while a plant, an animal, or a man is said to have a certain form. In ordinary speech, however, the words are often used synonymously. Forms may be natural or artificial. Every being in either inorganic nature or organic nature—plants, animals, and men—has

[2] Four such types of temperament are mentioned in Aristotelian psychology: the choleric, the phlegmatic, the sanguine, and the melancholic. Normal persons would ordinarily be blends of these types, so that the various qualities would balance one another. The old doctrine of temperaments received a new lease on life with the discovery of the influence of the endocrine glands on behavior. These glands are the basis of the behavior patterns outlined in the ancient division of temperaments and are the causes as well as the results of sensible alterations. Endocrine glands are not, however, the entire cause of an action; they are without doubt powerful influences, but they do not determine entirely the behavior of men. The role of man's spiritual faculties—of his intellect and free will—must be recognized.

by nature a certain specific form which characterizes it. The individuals within a species may be numberless, but they all have the distinctive shape of that species, they all conform to type. Artificial forms are the result of man's activity or of the forces of nature external to the being itself. Thus man takes the materials furnished by nature and arranges them into myriad forms; in fact, the result of most of man's activity is the changing of the accidental forms of the materials of nature. The forces of nature also are working continually to change the present forms of the world into others. So mountains will be raised, valleys dug, fertile plains destroyed, and the course of rivers changed. In all these changes the object has within itself the quality which enables it to acquire and retain a definite form.

The existence of qualities

The existence of qualities has been denied by the same modern materialistic scientists and philosophers who have denied the existence of substance, and on the same grounds. There is no place for either in the mechanistic conception of the universe. Matter and motion are the sum total of all reality. These men hold that the ultimate constituents of bodies are atoms or protons and electrons which are homogeneous in nature, differing only in size and shape. Whatever changes occur are the result of mechanical motion, and bring about among these ultimate material particles only a shift in local relations. Changes in bodies, therefore, can be explained by quantitative structure and local motion, both of which can be expressed in terms of quantity. All qualities, accordingly, can be reduced to quantity. Qualities as such do not exist because they cannot be perceived by the senses.

We have already disproved all these claims in the discussion of substance. They are based on the doctrine of sensism, which is manifestly false. Sense perception itself cannot be explained on purely quantitative terms, for sense perception is manifestly more than mere matter and motion. Quantitative changes assuredly accompany our perceptions, but they do not give a complete explanation of them. Perception is a process of cognition and it is surely something entirely different from the mere mechanical movements of material particles. Percepts are real affections of man's mental life and as such must be admitted to be qualities. They proceed from a principle in the mind itself and are distinct from the mere movement of material particles which accompany them. This is true *a fortiori* of our acts of thinking and willing, which, as is proved in psychology, proceed from the faculties of intellect and will. These faculties or powers must then be qualities in the sense understood by Aristotle.

Modern science admits the difficulty of reducing all qualitative concepts to quantitative ones and admits implicitly that qualities exist even in organic beings when it speaks of energy and chemical affinity. Both are qualities in the strict meaning of the term.

Characteristics of qualities

Qualities have some important characteristics which serve to distinguish them from other accidents. In the first place, most qualities have contraries. Contraries are positive realities which constitute extremes under the same genus and must therefore exist in different individual beings. If they exist in the same being, it must be at different times or under different aspects. Color, for example, is a quality which admits the extremes of black and white. The same thing cannot be both black and white at the same time and in all its parts. Cloth that is now white can be dyed black, but the same piece of cloth cannot be both black and white at the same time. Justice and injustice are contraries if we consider them as habits affecting the will. In the same act justice and injustice would be contradictories. So too knowledge and ignorance, love and hatred, are contrary habits or qualities.

All qualities except form and figure are susceptible of degrees. Knowledge and ignorance can be more or less, virtue and vice can be increased by habit and diminished by a contrary habit. Dispositions and indispositions may increase or decrease to a considerable degree; capacity or incapacity may be improved or debilitated.

Qualities also may be the foundation for the relation of similarity or dissimilarity. Things are said to be similar when the same kind of quality is present in both of them. Philosophers may be similar in their knowledge, animals may be similar in their behavior, stones may be similar or dissimilar in their texture.

Nature and kinds of relation

The nature of relations is one of the most important subjects in modern philosophy. It would on the one hand be a great error to deny that relations exist. There are on the other hand philosophers who maintain that relations are the only things that the mind can actually know. Relativism—the doctrine that we can know only relations—with its consequent implicit denial of the absolute, is a very common doctrine. It becomes of the utmost importance, then, to understand the true nature of relations in order to be able to defend Aristotelian doctrine against the attacks of both modern idealism and sensism.

Relation is defined as the bearing *(esse ad)* or reference of one thing to another. In order to constitute a relation three things are necessary: a subject, a term, and a foundation. The subject of the relation is the thing that is related to another. The term is the thing to which the subject is related. The foundation is the ground or reason why the subject is related to the term. It is evident that the subject, looked at from another point of view, can become the term of a relation. A creditor (the subject) is related to his debtor (the term) because he has lent him money (the foundation). The same debtor (now the subject) is related to the creditor because he has borrowed money.

It is evident that one thing alone can never constitute a relation; a relation can only exist between two or more things taken in reference to each other. The foundation is a necessary condition for a relation but it is not the relation itself. The foundation must of course be present in the subject and in the term, and it is because of this presence that each has a reference toward the other which constitutes the relation. The essence of the relation consists in the "being-toward," the reference of one thing to the other. For example, two white walls have a relation of similarity—they are similar in color. The foundation is their whiteness, and the relation is one of similarity. The relation is the result of the foundation, whiteness, found in both of them. The relation must therefore be distinct at least in concept from the foundation, the subject, and the term.

There are two kinds of relations, logical and real. A *logical* relation is one that depends on the activity of the mind. The foundation for such a relation is a logical being; there is no real foundation in things themselves. Examples of logical relation are that between a subject and its predicate, between a genus and its species, between an arbitrary sign and the thing it signifies. The subject and predicate are related as to their extension and comprehension as was explained in logic. Between premises and conclusion in a syllogism there is a relation of consequence or inference. The arrangements of our ideas, such as that into genus and species, are logical relations. Words as arbitrary signs of ideas and things are logically related to those ideas and things. The relations between a red light and danger, between a flag and one's country, or between a trade-mark and the article for which it is used, are logical relations.

A *real* relation is one which exists in things themselves independently of the operation of the mind. The following conditions are required for a real relation: The subject of the relation must be real, the term must be real, and the foundation must be real and really distinct from the term. The subject and the term of a real relation must also be distinct from each other. No being can have a real relation by itself; it must look toward another being.

Such a relation exists between parent and child, between brother and sister, between two houses of the same type, between two walls of the same color. Real relations may be either essential or accidental. An essential relation is one in which it is the nature or essence of the being to have a certain relation. The relations of the creature to the Creator, of the soul to the body, of the intellect to truth, and of the will to good are essential relations. An accidental relation is one which is only contingently in the subject. It is not the essence of the being but is based on an accidental quality which could be present or not without affecting the essence. The relation of similarity between two white walls or of equality of strength between two athletes is an accidental relation.

The foundation of relations

Every reality has a relation of some kind toward other realities, and there must be a foundation or basis for this relation. Substance, for example, contains foundations for identity and diversity, similarity, dissimilarity, and equality: two men are identical in species, while an animal and a man are diverse; men may be similar or dissimilar in intellectual gifts, and so on. Quantity contains the foundation of the relation of equality and inequality: some things have the same weight, size, or shape as other things, while they differ from still other beings in these very same respects. Quality contains foundations for the relation of similarity and dissimilarity: things are similar or dissimilar in their habits, capacities, or reactions. Action and passion are the foundations for the relations of cause and effect: every action comes from a cause and produces an effect (reaction), and the two are thus related. The same is true of the other categories, time, place, posture, and habitus. These furnish foundations in objects for various relations of distance and position, similarity and dissimilarity.

The absolute and the relative

It has become a fashion in modern philosophy, as has been mentioned several times in preceding chapters, to consider all things as relative. Materialism and idealism are at one in rejecting the absolute, or at least the knowledge of it, which amounts to the same thing. According to sensist philosophers like Hume, Mill, and Spencer, we can know only our own ideas (by which they mean sensations), and therefore we have no knowledge of any other reality. The doctrine of Kant rejects the knowledge of the absolute and also the knowledge of the relative, except as an *a-priori* form which we have no right to attribute to the things in themselves. Herbert Spencer and Sir William Hamilton are alike in rejecting all knowledge of the absolute and insisting that all being and all knowledge are only relative.

Aristotelian and scholastic thought, on the other hand, maintain the existence and knowability of the absolute, as well as of the relative. A thing is absolute when it can be thought of without thinking of another thing to which it has a reference. A being is relative when it cannot be thought of without at the same time thinking of the other being to which it is related. Such concepts as father, friend, husband, and so forth are relative concepts; such concepts as man, house, and dog are absolute concepts.

Thus it is obvious that things must be absolute before they can be relative; that is, they must be something in themselves, before they can have a reference to other things. All created being is, therefore, both absolute and relative. There is no contradiction in this because they are such under different aspects, not under the same aspect.

We do not deny, when we insist on the absoluteness of being, that all created beings are also in a true and real sense relative. They are contingent beings, dependent on God as the first cause. Strictly speaking, it could be said that God is the only entirely absolute being, since He is the only being who is without dependence on any other being. But in a less strict sense all created being can be called absolute because it has its own reality independently of other created beings.

The knowledge of the absolute is prior to the knowledge of the relative because we must first know the subject and the term of a relation before we can know the relation itself; the knowledge of them as absolute is presupposed to the knowledge of them as relative. Two walls, for instance, are related by being similar in color. We must first know each wall individually as a distinct entity of a certain color before we can become aware of their similarity in color, of their relation; we must first know them absolutely in themselves before we can recognize any similarity which may exist between them.

Considering the correlatives formally as such, they are simultaneous in knowledge; that is, the knowledge of one extreme as relative always and simultaneously involves the knowledge of the other extreme as a correlative. For example, it is impossible to know a son as a son without knowing that he has a father. Correlatives are also simultaneous in nature; that is, considered as related things they must by nature exist together. One extreme cannot exist without the other, formally considered. Obviously, the father must exist as a human being before his son, but as father the relationship to a son begins at the time his son is born, and not before. Hence no relative term formally considered can be defined without bringing the correlative term into the definition, since correlatives cannot exist or be understood except in reference to each other.

The existence of real relations

The same adversaries whom we have cited above as denying the existence of the absolute obviously would also deny the existence of real relations. To this group would be added all monistic idealists, such as Fichte, Schelling, Hegel, and a great number of their followers, who contend that our knowledge itself constitutes whatever reality there is.

The proof for the existence of real relations in the world is found in the order which exists between the parts of the world among themselves, in the relationship of the parts of the world to the whole world, and in the relationship of the whole world and all its parts individually to the Creator. This proof may be stated formally as follows: Real relations exist if independently of all intellectual operations and comparisons many varieties of order and reference exist in the world; but this is true both of the essential and the accidental order; therefore real relations, both essential and accidental, are facts of the existing order. The minor is clear from examples. An essential order exists between the creature and the Creator, between an accident and its substance, between soul and body in man; an accidental order or reference exists between two white walls, between two learned men, between a friend and his friend, between a father and his son.

A second proof can be found in the fact of active production in nature. Every effect really depends upon its cause; but this dependence is first of all a true relation, secondly a real relation (that is, entirely independent of the action of the mind) and finally, an accidental relation because in many effects the dependence on this particular cause is entirely accidental—the effect could have been brought about in many other ways. The relation between cause and effect in individual cases is then a real relation of an accidental kind.

Other examples could be given almost without end. The scientific classification of plants and animals is based upon structural similarity, which is without doubt a fact of nature and constitutes a real relation between these plants and animals. The physical sciences teach that all beings in the universe are constantly in motion, drawn toward each other by the powers of gravitation. This implies a real relation between these objects with regard to distance, position, and relative motion. And finally, all the people of the world have numberless relations with one another in the family, the nation, and in all kinds of societies great and small. Men have cultural, social, and religious relationships; they have commercial and diplomatic ties; industrial and agricultural agreements; contracts for peace or war and internal relationships of governing and governed. All of these constitute real relations among real people. If the world is a real world, real relationships exist in it. It is impossible that real beings should exist without real relationships being established among them.

The nature of the reality of real relations

We have explained previously that in real relations the foundation of the relation must be real and really distinct from the term of the relation. Another question which has been much discussed is the nature of the distinction between the relation itself and the foundation on which it rests. As we have said before, a real relation results from the common foundation in both extremes, and therefore there must be some distinction between them. The foundation as the ground or reason of the relation is always some substance or accident, a reality having being in itself or in another. The relation, formally considered, has only a being toward something *(esse ad)*. Between the relation itself, therefore, and its foundation there must be some distinction, real or logical.

A real distinction between the relation and its foundation is held by some Thomists. This would mean that the relation is an accidental being or mode which is added to the being of the foundation in both extremes. In the relation of similarity between two white walls, for instance, similarity would be a new mode added to the accident, whiteness, in both extremes.

Most scholastics hold that the distinction is a logical one with an imperfect foundation in the things. In that case there would be no new being or mode added to the foundation, but the similarity would be a reality identical with the quality of whiteness in both extremes.

The arguments against the addition of a new entity in a relation—that is, against the real distinction—are interesting and instructive. If there is a real distinction between the relation and its foundation, whenever a new relation comes into being two new entities are added to the extremes, and whenever a relation ceases two entities are taken away. This would mean a real change occurring in both extremes, and this change would require positive action and positive causality affecting both extremes. But it is rather obvious that real relations are acquired or lost without a real change occurring in both extremes. Therefore there can be no real mode added to both extremes, and there is no real distinction between a relation and its foundation in both extremes. Suppose someone likes the color of a neighbor's living room and has hers done in the same color. Is there any new entity added to her neighbor's walls because she has hers done in a similar fashion and there is now a relation of similarity between them? Of course not. Accordingly, the new relation does not mean any new entity in one of the extremes, and therefore there is no real distinction between the relation and the foundation, at least in that extreme.

Another example could be taken from the relation between substance and accident. If the relation added two new modes to the extremes, then these two new entities would give rise to two new relations to the substance, and these two to two others, and so on to infinity. Thus there would be an infinite number of entities or modes in every substance if each relation established a new entity or mode. But this is obviously absurd, and therefore there cannot be a real distinction between the relation and its foundation. And finally, if the supposition were true, another infinity would be added to this infinity of new modes or entities. It is a fact that every individual being in the universe and every atom of every being have relations of identity or diversity, of equality or inequality, of similarity or dissimilarity with every other being and every other atom in the universe. By merely changing position I would add an infinity of modes to every being in the universe. But this is incredible and fantastic; therefore there is no real entity added by the existence of relations.

It must be true, then, that the distinction between relation and foundation is only a logical or mental one and that the being of the relation and that of the foundation are in reality identical. The distinction, however, has a foundation in reality. The foundation is thought of as that reality because of which the relation exists between the things; the relation is thought of as that which arises out of the foundation. The foundation is twofold, being in each of the extremes; the relation is only one. The foundation for the relation of similarity between the two white walls exists in the walls themselves; the relation exists between the walls and is the reference of the one to the other. The twofold foundation is the ground or reason for the relation, and hence there is a foundation for the distinction in the things, but it is only an imperfect foundation.

SUMMARY OF CHAPTER XIV

1 **Nature of a quality.** Quality is the first categorical accident which is treated in ontology. Many of the other accidents are treated in other branches of philosophy. Quality is an accident following the form, and may be defined as an absolute accident completing and determining a substance in its being and in its operations. According to Aristotle there are four types of qualities: habit and disposition; capacity and incapacity; affective quality and affection; form and figure.

2 **Habit and disposition.** A habit is a quality, stable and difficult to remove, disposing a thing well or ill in its being or in its operations. A disposition is a relatively transient quality of the same nature. Operative habits are acquired by the repetition of acts. The intellect and will of man are the primary subjects of habits. Other faculties are secondarily so. There are natural habits, such as the habit of principles in general and of moral principles in particular. A habit is always an ontological and physical good, even though it may lead to moral evil.

3 **Other divisions of quality.** By natural capacity we mean a proximate accidental principle of operation in a being. An incapacity is a faculty in an unfit condition for operation. Affective qualities and affections are qualities which produce or result from some sensible alteration. An affective quality is relatively permanent; an affection is temporary in character. Prominent among affective qualities is temperament. According to Aristotle there are four different types

of temperament, the normal person being a blend of all four. Form or figure is the quality of a body resulting from the arrangement of its quantitative parts. Forms may be natural or artificial.

4 **The existence of qualities.** Materialists deny the existence of qualities, just as they deny the existence of substance and explain all things as matter in motion. But the existence of qualities is easily proved. Even sense perception cannot be explained on purely quantitative terms, much less the actions of the intellect and the spiritual will. They are all much more than the movements of mechanical particles which accompany them. In fact, modern science admits the existence of qualities when it talks of energy and chemical affinity.

5 **Characteristics of quality.** Most qualities have contraries, such as knowledge and ignorance in the intellect and love and hatred in the will. All qualities except form and figure are susceptible of degrees. Qualities are the foundation of relations, especially of relations of similarity and dissimilarity.

6 **Nature and kinds of relation.** A relation is the bearing or reference of one thing to another. Three things are necessary to constitute a relation: the subject, the term, and the foundation. Relations are either real or logical. A logical relation is one that depends on the activity of the mind, such as that between the subject and predicate of a proposition. A real relation is one that exists in things themselves independently of the operation of the mind. A real relation may be either essential or accidental. The foundation of a relation is the reason why one thing is related to another. All the categories can furnish foundations for relations.

7 **The absolute and the relative.** Materialism and idealism reject the existence of the absolute, or at least the knowl-

edge of it, which amounts to practically the same thing. A thing is absolute when it can be thought of without thinking of another thing to which it may have a reference. A being is relative when it cannot be thought of without at the same time thinking of the other being to which it is related. It is obvious that a thing must be absolute, something in itself, before it can be relative, something which has a reference to another. The knowledge of the absolute as a being is prior to the knowledge of the relative. Correlatives formally as such are, nevertheless, simultaneous in knowledge as well as in nature.

8 **Existence of real relations.** The existence of real relations is denied by materialists and idealists alike. Yet their existence is easily established; the proof is obvious. Real relations are a part of the order which exists in the world and between the world and its Creator. That order is partly essential and partly accidental, giving rise to the two kinds of real relation. A second proof can be found in the fact of active production in nature. Between the cause and the thing produced there is a relation. Other reasons could be given, such as the scientific classification of plants and animals based upon their similarity, which is a real relation. Motion implies a relation of distance, position, and kind among real things. And finally, all the people of the world are related in some way or other, some in a remote way and some in a very intimate manner.

9 **Nature of the reality of real relations.** A relation is not a new mode added to the being of the foundation in both extremes, and consequently there is no real distinction between the relation and its foundation, as some Thomists contend. If it were so, things would be really changed without any action upon them, merely by the presence of a similar object. Also, an infinite number of realities would

exist in order to explain the relation between substance and accident. Finally, a change in the position of one being would have to be said to add a new entity to every other being in the universe. But all this is incredible and fantastic. "Beings are not to be multiplied without necessity." The distinction, then, must be only logical with an imperfect foundation in things. The foundation for the relation is twofold; the relation is singular. One (the foundation) is the *esse in,* the other (the relation) is the *esse ad.*

CHAPTER XV

ACTION AND PASSION; CAUSE AND EFFECT

WE spoke of the nature of cause and effect previously when we discussed the fundamental principles of being and also when we considered the nature of change. In this chapter on the fifth and sixth of the Aristotelian categories—action and passion—it will be necessary to discuss these problems at greater length. We have seen that the Eleatics in denying change altogether and Heraclitus in insisting that everything was change were both wrong, and that Aristotle's explanation that changes occur in a relatively stable world was the true one. This was the foundation of his fundamental doctrine of potency and act. The changes are the result of action, of operative potency, and they are accompanied by reaction or passion, the result of which is a new perfection or act. The active agent in the process is the cause, and the result of the activity is the effect. In finite beings, then, action always implies a change, and change implies causality. The agent is the cause, the action of the agent producing the change is one of causality; the change produced in the patient by the reaction is the effect. The cause here understood is an efficient cause, the kind of causality most easily recognized and most generally admitted. There are also other kinds of causality, which we shall speak of presently. These are formal, material, and final causality. All other kinds can be reduced to these four.

Whenever a change takes place it proceeds from the action of an operative potency. By means of this action the agent produces a change in itself or in another. The reception of the action is called reaction or passion, and the recipient is called the patient or reagent. Every change presupposes an active potentiality in the agent and a passive potentiality in the patient. The change is produced by the active potentiality and is received by the passive potentiality, which is thus reduced to act. The change as it proceeds from the agent is the action; the same change as it is received by the patient is the reaction or passion.

Action is of two kinds, transient and immanent. In transient actions the agent and the patient are beings really distinct from each other; the ball is thrown by the boy, the house is built by the man. In immanent actions the agent and the patient are really the same being and there is between them only a logical distinction with a foundation in reality. In man nutrition, sense perception, thinking, and willing are all immanent activities which actualize the potencies of man's nature by producing their proper results. The action is really distinct from the operative potency and from the agent, since it comes and goes while they remain permanently. For example, the act of thinking is produced by the faculty of the intellect, which itself is a permanent operative potency of the soul.

The distinction between cause and principle

A cause may be defined as something which in any way whatever exerts a positive influence on the production of a thing. Three factors enter into the concept of cause: that which is the agent of production, or the cause; that which is produced, or the effect; and the influence of the cause on the effect, or the causality. Without this positive influence there would be no cause in the strict sense. The action of a cause consists in bringing a substantial or accidental thing from a state of potentiality to a state of actuality with regard to a certain perfection.

A principle, on the other hand, is that from which something proceeds in any manner whatever. It is evident from our discussion of principles in Chapter 5 that there is a difference between a principle and a cause. Every cause is a principle but not every principle is a cause—there are logical principles which do not enter into the production of a thing. The concept of principle is therefore wider than that of cause. In fact, a cause might also be accurately defined as a principle of production.

Kinds of causes

Aristotelian philosophy holds as one of its most important and fundamental doctrines the existence of four kinds of causes, material, formal, efficient, and final. Many modern scientists and philosophers, on the contrary, will admit the existence of efficient causality only—if, indeed, they accept the idea of cause at all. For example, the theory of mechanism, which maintains that there is only matter and motion in the universe, that the ultimate constituent particles of matter are homogeneous, and that all change is produced by purely mechanical forces by means of local motion, finds no place for final causes, for it denies the existence of purpose in nature. From the fundamental position of this theory it is evident that it would likewise deny the existence of material and formal causes.

Let us analyze the ideas of change and efficient causality according to the mind of Aristotle and elaborate the reasons why he and the scholastic philosophers without exception insist on the existence of four causes.

We saw in discussing the nature of change that there must be something which remains constant and something which is changeable—that, in other words, all finite being is composite in its nature. There must, therefore, be two intrinsic principles which contribute to the constitution of such a finite being: the one is constant, passive, and determinable, the material cause; the other is changing, active, and determining, the formal cause. Changes in material beings can be of two kinds, accidental and substantial. An accidental change is one in which only the accidental form is changed, as, for example, takes place when a piece of wood is carved into a statue. A substantial change is one in which the substance itself undergoes a transformation. Such a change occurs, for instance, when uranium is changed into radium. In this case a new substantial form is added to the prime matter, which is the first constituent principle of all material beings. Uranium and radium are not prime matter *(materia prima)* but second matter, actually existing substances.

There must also be something to start the process of change and direct it; there must be some agent. By his action the agent produces the effect, changing the material from what it was to what it is to be. This is obviously efficient causality.

Lastly, there must be the end or purpose for the sake of which the process is initiated. For example, when we see a man taking exercise regularly, we may ask, "Why does he take exercise?" The answer, "For the sake of his health," satisfies us because it enables us to understand the reason for his action. The reason for which a thing is done is its final cause.

In his analysis of the four causes of Aristotle, St. Thomas explains the reasons why there are just four causes, no more and no less. He says that a cause is something on which the production of a being depends. This produced being can be considered in two ways. If we take it absolutely, the cause of the being, making it to be what it is intrinsically, is its form or formal cause. If we consider it as a being in potency, two factors are necessary to reduce it from potency to act. There must be a material factor which is reduced from potency to act, the material cause, and there must be an agent which by means of its action brings about the change, the efficient cause. An agent, however, can act only according to the tendency of its own determined nature; and since this tendency implies a definite end or purpose, this purpose also influences the production of the produced being, and this is the final cause.

There are, then, four questions and only four which require an answer in order to explain the how and why of a being. If we ask, "By what *(a quo)* is it made?" the answer is "By its efficient cause." If we ask, "From what or out of what *(ex quo)* is it made?" the answer is "Out of its material cause." If we ask, "Through what, by means of what, what is it that constitutes its nature intrinsically? *(per quid)*" the answer is "Its formal cause." And if we ask, "On account of what *(propter quid)* is it made?" the answer is "For the reason which induced the agent to act," the final cause. These four answers give us a complete explanation of the nature and existence of the being, and therefore they are the determining factors in its existence.

There is no form of causality which cannot be brought under these four heads. The so-called exemplary cause *(causa exemplaris)*, for instance—the ideal or model in the mind of the intelligent agent—may be regarded as an extrinsic formal cause, or as an efficient cause because it helps the agent in his work, or as a final cause because it represents the good to be attained. The objects of our knowledge are truly causes of our knowledge; they may be considered as efficient causes of that knowledge because they determine the activity of our faculties or as final causes because they are the aim and purpose of that knowledge. The essence of the soul is the final cause of its faculties, since the purpose of the faculties is to perfect the soul; or the essence of the soul could be considered the material cause of the faculties, in a broad sense, because it is that which supports and constitutes them. So-called instrumental causes, which are set in motion by the prime agent and assist in the accomplishment of the act, also fall under the notion of efficient causality; such, for example, are the reduction of superfluous flesh, drugs, surgical instruments, and blood transfusions, all of which are means toward accomplishing the end of good health for the individual.

The term *cause* is used analogously of the four causes rather than univocally, since it is obvious that, while they all contribute to the production of the effect, the causal influence is widely different in each case.

Material cause and formal cause

The division of causes into material, formal, efficient, and final was based on what Aristotle observed with regard to the changes in nature. He denied both the doctrine of the Eleatics, who looked upon reality as unchangeable, and that of Heraclitus, who taught that all was change and that there was no permanent reality. Aristotle held that reality was both actual and potential, and that one was continually changing into the other. He admitted the existence of real being and of real change, and explained both permanence and change by his doctrines of potency and act and of material and formal causes. The potential cannot become actual by its own power; therefore the influence of the efficient cause is needed to reduce the potential to actuality. And since in nature there are regularity and uniformity in the effects which add to the perfection of nature, he saw in that perfection the final cause of the activity of natural forces. But in order to have a change there must be a potentiality for such a change in the things of nature; this potentiality is the material cause, to which corresponds the formal cause or the actuality which realizes and fulfills the potentiality.

On this reasoning Aristotle based his theory of matter and form or hylomorphism, which teaches that all corporeal being is composed of prime matter *(materia prima)* and substantial form *(forma substantialis);* this theory was opposed especially to the mechanical systems of the atomists, who regarded material substances as mere aggregations of simple unchangeable elements endowed with local motion. According to Aristotle's doctrine every material substance is essentially composite but is still a substantial unity *(unum per se)*. Different material substances are not merely different arrangements of the same elements, but each substance has its own specific nature. A substance has both passive potencies and active powers. By its active powers it works toward the accomplishment of its own perfection and the carrying out of the order of the universe. This working toward a purpose or final cause is not impressed on the material substance by external necessity, but is the carrying out of an inherent tendency, the presence of which is manifested by the activities of the substance.

For material substance to be thus directed by inherent tendencies toward the accomplishment of its own determined purpose there must be in each substance, besides the material constituent, another principle which determines the specific nature of the substance and the direction of its activities toward a certain definite end. Material substances are, therefore, composed of two intrinsic principles: the material principle which is the same for all, called prime matter; and the determining principle, which is proper to each, called substantial form. Matter and form are essential parts of a material substance; their union constitutes the essence of material substance. They are therefore constituent and substantial parts of every material substance. They are not, however, complete or second matter capable of existing by themselves, but incomplete substances which by their union constitute a complete or second material substance. They are substantial parts—not accidental parts—of the complete substance.

A few examples will perhaps make this matter clearer. The concepts of prime matter and substantial form depend on the concept of substantial change. A substantial change alters the very nature and substance of a thing. A plant, for instance, absorbs various elements from the soil, the air, and the sun and changes them into living matter. They are united in an organic compound and perform the functions of a living being. Such a change must be substantial, for nonliving elements have now become living, and the difference between living and nonliving things is more than a mere accidental difference. Animals assimilate inorganic and organic elements from plants and by the process of digestion change them into animal tissue. Again such a change is a substantial one, since what is living and sentient is substantially different from a thing that is living but not sentient. The reverse process which takes place when an organism decays and a living being dies is also a substantial change.

Prime matter is therefore a true cause, the material cause, that out of which something is made. Substantial form is also a true cause, for it is that through which or by means of which something is constituted in its specific nature. Prime matter and substantial form are correlative, constituent principles of the composite substance. Matter and form are intrinsic causes: they are essential incomplete substances which together make up the complete corporeal being. These intrinsic causes are one of the main subjects of study in cosmology, which investigates the nature and constitution of physical bodies. In ontology we treat at greater length the two extrinsic causes, efficient and final, which are causes external to the being itself and are common to both immaterial substance and material substance.

Efficient cause and final cause

Change is produced by means of action; a being of one kind is changed into a being of another kind by the active influence of another being according to the principle that "Whatever is changed, is changed by another." The agency by which the change is produced is the efficient cause. It can be defined, therefore, as that by whose action something is produced. The thing produced is a new act or form, substantial or accidental. Of the causes which assist in the production of the effect, the efficient cause is the one that most obviously exerts a positive influence on the existence of the new perfection. A house is not built merely by taking thought, an automobile will not run without gas, a field will not be plowed merely by wishing it to be so. And so it is in all nature. Whenever any real production takes place, there must be some agent responsible for it; that agent is called the efficient cause.

In all changes made by finite beings there must be some pre-existing material which undergoes the process of becoming; the finite being can be only the cause of a change in material already in existence *(in esse)*. But efficient causality is not restricted to finite beings. The action of God in creating is also an exercise of efficient causality, and one of a higher order since He is the cause *in esse,* the cause of the being itself of that which comes into existence. The change in this case is from nonexistence to existence without any previously existing material. This transition is one from possibility or objective potency to actual existence, whereas in changes wrought by finite agents there must be passive subjective potency in order that the new being may come into existence.

The final cause or purpose is that for the sake of which an efficient cause acts. The purpose or intention determines the action and the kind of action of the efficient cause, and therefore may be said to be first in the order of causality. The idea of a purpose involves the idea of a plan and the selection of means proper to attain that purpose. The efficient cause is the means to the end and is set to work by the final cause, the end or purpose.

That man's actions have purpose or finality is a necessity of his rational nature. Action without purpose is irrational. That the final cause or purpose is a true cause is seen in all of man's actions. Does the artist buy bronze, have it delivered to his studio, and labor for several years to change it without any clear idea of what he is trying to do? Certainly not; rather he has in his mind a definite idea of the finished work and he is filled with the hope that this time he will produce something really worth while for the benefit of posterity. Final cause, then, may be said to be the most important of all causes, as well as first in the order of time.

SUMMARY OF CHAPTER XV

1 **Nature of cause and effect.** Changes occur in things by means of action and reaction or passion, the fifth and sixth of Aristotle's categories. They are the basis of causality. Change proceeds from an operative potency. The exercise of this potency is called action. The reception of the action in the subject is called reaction or passion. The change consists in the actualization of the passive potentiality of the subject. A cause is that which in any way whatever exerts a positive influence in the production of a thing. A principle is that from which something proceeds in any manner whatever. Every cause is a principle but not every principle is a cause, since there are logical principles which do not produce anything. A cause is, therefore, a principle of production.

2 **The main kinds of causes.** Aristotle distinguished four main kinds of causes: material, formal, efficient, and final. These four causes explain the existence and the nature of any being. The material cause is that out of which something is made. The formal cause is that through which a being is constituted in its specific nature. The efficient cause is the agent by whose action something is made. The final cause or purpose is the reason on account of which something comes into existence.

3 **The material and formal causes.** Changes can be either accidental or substantial. In accidental changes the new accidental form comes to a being already constituted in its specific nature; thus, when a statue is made from bronze,

the bronze takes on a new accidental form, second matter. In substantial changes the substantial form unites with prime matter to constitute a new specific nature, as when uranium is changed to radium. The theory of matter and form, the hylomorphic theory, is that prime matter and substantial form are the constitutive substantial principles of every composite material substance, determining its specific nature.

4 **The efficient and final causes.** The efficient cause is that by the action of which something is produced. It is the action of the agent or the efficient cause which most obviously produces the resulting perfection. Finite beings change existing material substances; the infinite can produce the being itself without any pre-existing material. The change from objective potency to actual existence is called creation, a kind of efficient causality. The final cause is that for the sake of which an efficient cause acts. It is the purpose or intention of the agent and determines the action of the efficient cause. It is first in the order of causality.

CHAPTER XVI

EFFICIENT CAUSALITY

IN order to understand more completely the concept of efficient causality, which was explained in summary fashion in the last chapter, it is necessary to distinguish it carefully from two other concepts, that of condition and that of occasion.

A condition is something that is required in order that an efficient cause may act but that does not contribute any positive influence toward the production of the effect itself. Clear weather is a condition for effective bombing, as it is also for good baseball, but the weather does not drop the bombs nor play the game. If the condition is so necessary that the efficient cause cannot under any circumstances produce the effect without it, it is called a *conditio sine qua non,* a condition without which the cause cannot act. For example, light is such a condition for the act of seeing, but although it is absolutely required, it is still not a cause; it is not the light but the eyes that produce the act of seeing. A condition may help the action of the cause by way of preparing for it, putting it in better condition, or facilitating the action itself. It may also merely remove some hindrance to the action, as when a person's feet are untied so that he may walk.

An occasion is a circumstance which affords the efficient cause a better opportunity to act. The period before an election is an occasion for what is called oratory by the charitable. A tavern is an occasion for men to get drunk. There is a difference between an occasion and a condition which is not always easy to see in a particular case. A condition is required for the action of the efficient cause; an occasion is not a requirement for action but a circumstance which gives an opportunity for action. Thus the presence of the man in the tavern gives him the opportunity of obtaining liquor, and the tavern is therefore an occasion of his drunkenness; the possession of the liquor is required for intoxication and is therefore a condition. The man himself, by actually drinking the liquor, is the efficient cause of his intoxication.

The principle of causality

We have discussed some general notions about the principle of sufficient reason and the principle of causality in a previous chapter. They are taken up again here because they are connected with the Aristotelian categories of action and passion. The principle of sufficient reason may be stated as follows: *Everything must have a sufficient reason for its being or existence,* or *There is nothing without a sufficient reason.* The principle of causality is a declaration of the necessity of an efficient cause. It is expressed thus: *Whatever passes from a state of nonexistence into a state of existence must have an efficient cause for its existence,* or, more briefly, *Nothing begins to exist without a cause.* The principle of sufficient reason is wider in scope than the principle of causality, which is concerned only with a thing beginning to exist or a contingent being. The principle of sufficient reason applies to the order of essences, the order of existence, and the order of knowledge. Nothing is what it is, nothing exists, nothing is an object of knowledge, unless there is something either in itself or in another which is completely sufficient to account for its essence, its existence, or its cognoscibility.

Both principles are evident. The principle of sufficient reason follows immediately from the nature of being and from the principle of contradiction. Being is opposed to nothing. To say that a being has a sufficient reason for itself is to say that a being has something in itself by which it is opposed to nonbeing and by which it may be distinguished from it; that is, it has a reason why it is a being rather than nothing. If a reason why it is opposed to nonbeing were not required for a thing to be a real being, it would follow that it could be a being and a nonbeing under the same respect, which would be a violation of the principle of contradiction.

In the same way the principle of causality is an immediate consequence of the principle of sufficient reason. When anything begins to exist, there must be a sufficient reason why it begins to exist. Now, this reason must be in the being itself or in some other being. But it cannot be in the thing itself, since it is only a possible being. If a possible being were to give itself existence, it would have to produce itself; but a merely possible being cannot produce anything, least of all itself. To produce itself it would have to act before it existed, which is obviously impossible and contradictory. Therefore the reason for its beginning to be must be in some other being. If this other being by its power and influence did not determine the coming into existence of the possible being, it would have no relation to it and could not be the reason for its existence. Hence this other being must exert a real physical influence on the possible being. A being which exerts such an influence is by definition an efficient cause of the first being.

A great number of modern scientists seem to reject or at least doubt the truth of the principle of causality as we have explained and defended it. A more careful examination of their writings, however, leads one to the conclusion that there is a misunderstanding of the position of Aristotle and the scholastics rather than a disagreement with their doctrine. For modern scientists the principle of causality means something entirely different from what we have been discussing. What they have reference to might better be called the principle of predictability or of necessary causation. What they call the principle of causality may be stated in this way: When a future event can be predicted with perfect certainty from the nature of a previous event—that is, from the scientific knowledge of the physical causes at work in the case—there is a causal connection, the first set of facts being the cause of the second set of facts. The predictability or necessary causation of the future event is the test or criterion of causality. If one can be absolutely certain that one particular event will follow from another particular event, then the latter is the cause of the former, and that is what is meant by causality. The scientist attempts to deduce the occurrence of a future event from the existence of a present set of circumstances so that he may be able to conclude from this cause to that effect. The question for him is: The cause being given, what effect must follow necessarily and can, therefore, be predicted by science? The principle of causality of Aristotle, on the other hand, proceeds from effect to cause: If a being passes from nonexistence to existence, it must have had an adequate cause to bring it into existence. The scientist is interested in knowing whether or not he can deduce a particular effect from a particular cause; the philosopher is merely trying to find out when a particular event takes place whether or not it must have something to account for its taking place. The arguments of scientists as to whether or not a specific event can be predicted accurately from a previous particular set of facts do not touch at all the traditional view of philosophy that nothing happens without a sufficient cause. While this is the truth of the matter, it must be admitted that metaphysical principles such as the one we have been discussing are not looked upon with any great respect by the modern scientific world, the world of scientism.

Some axioms on efficient causation

There are several axioms on causation which require some notice here, if only because they are so often repeated. They have, moreover, a real usefulness in being short cuts to an understanding of something that would take much time to explain. The first of these axioms is one of which we have already had occasion to speak several times before: *Action flows from being*. It is expressed in various ways in Latin: *Operari sequitur esse; Qualis est operatio, talis est natura; Modus operandi sequitur modum essendi.* Operative powers proceed from the nature of a being, and therefore we can know the nature by studying the operations. We know what a thing is by what it does. This is one of the most important principles of Aristotelian philosophy. Our knowledge of the nature of things is based on our knowledge of their activities. We have no other key to the knowledge of what a thing is than our knowledge of what it does. If we could not reason from effects to cause, no knowledge would be possible, for knowledge must at least begin in that fashion.

Another axiom is that there must be a proportion between effect and cause. The effect cannot exceed in actual perfection the power and being of the cause. The scholastics expressed this in the axiom: *Nemo dat quod non habet—No one can give what he does not have.* The formula means simply that no being can give to or produce in another being an act or perfection which it does not have in itself either actually or virtually.

Finally there is the corollary of the preceding axiom: *Omne agens agit simile sibi,* or *Every agent produces something similar to itself*. This has special reference to natural operations in the organic world. Living organisms reproduce only their own kind. Since action depends on the nature of the agent, the agent can produce only certain definite effects; to do otherwise would be contrary to its nature. The effect, therefore, must resemble the cause, must be according to the nature of the cause.

Kinds of efficient causality

We have remarked already that efficient causality is a complicated subject and gives rise to a number of classifications. We shall consider a few of the more necessary and more important divisions and leave the others for fuller treatment in other branches of philosophy.

The first cause is one whose causality is absolutely independent of any other cause and on which all other causality depends. We shall see in natural theology that the first cause must be the infinite being, God. All other beings owe whatever they have of reality to Him and are, therefore, dependent on Him for their being as well as their causality. A second cause is one which is dependent on some other cause for its causality. All finite and creatural beings are second causes.

A physical cause is one which produces the effect by its own action, as the boy who throws a ball and the boy who studies his philosophy. A moral cause is one which induces a free agent to act. This may be done by threats, by counsel, by persuasion, and so forth. Parents are often moral causes of their children's actions; a blackmailer is a moral cause of the giving of a bribe.

A principal cause is an efficient cause which produces an effect by virtue of its own power. An instrumental cause is an efficient cause which produces an effect by virtue of the power of another cause, the principal one. These two kinds of causes are correlatives, and one implies the other. A hunter, for example, shoots a duck with a rifle: the rifle is the instrumental cause, and the hunter is the principal cause.

Adversaries of efficient causality

Phenomenalists in general deny the existence of efficient cause. They assert that cause is an obscure metaphysical notion without any foundation whatever in objective reality. We have only one kind of knowledge, sense perception, and the senses can know only the phenomena or appearances of things, not their real nature in themselves. The senses perceive one thing following upon another in place and time, their local and temporal sequences, and that is all the knowledge we can have of them. The mind without any justification whatever imagines a causal connection between these events and considers that one is the cause or producing agent and the other the result of the action or the effect. These philosophers maintain that to posit the necessity of causality is to take the facts as they are, the existence of antecedent and consequent appearances as they are reported by the senses, and to impress on them a subjective interpretation as to their real nature. They insist that such a knowledge of the real nature of things is utterly impossible for any of the faculties which we possess. This is the general position of John Locke, David Hume, John Stuart Mill, and the whole sensist and phenomenalist schools.

The doctrine of Immanuel Kant and his myriad disciples in the modern world is only verbally different from sensism and phenomenalism. For them a knowledge of causes is also impossible, since these causes, if they existed, would be things-in-themselves, and the mind cannot know such things but only their appearances. In the philosophy of Kant causality is one of the categories, and is therefore an *a-priori* mental form into which our judgments are fitted. It has, accordingly, only subjective value and tells us nothing of things themselves as they exist in nature. If we place a causal connection between two things, it is only by subjective necessity, and the idea is not derived from experience in any way.

Occasionalists, such as Malebranche, Geulincx, and others, deny the efficient causality of creatures and admit it only of the infinite, God. Their doctrine follows from the excessive dualism of Descartes and makes the activity of creatures only an appearance: God as first cause is the only real source of activity. As second causes creatures are only the instruments of the first cause.

Regardless of all these doctrines, it can be proved that the concept of efficient cause is objectively valid and based on the facts as found in experience; and if we refuse to acknowledge that consciousness is a valid source of knowledge of experience, the only alternative is universal skepticism, which is a contradictory doctrine, a denial of all knowledge and of all science, and an admission of their impossibility.

Proof of efficient causality

The first proof of the reality of efficient causality is from internal evidence, the testimony of consciousness. From this source of truth we are aware that we produce many and varied changes in our mind, in our body, and in things outside of us, and that in particular our will can set in motion or stop many of the members of our body. Now, all these changes are real beings, new entities. But a principle which produces something is a true cause of the thing that is produced. Therefore, by the testimony of consciousness we come to the knowledge of an efficient cause and we distinguish it clearly from a mere succession of events.

Another proof is from external experience. The notion of cause is objectively real (1) if we know it to be true in objective fact that physical things really begin to be on account of the actions of other physical things and (2) if our minds can deduce the notion of true causality from our knowledge of phenomena. But both these things are true. Therefore the notion of causality is objectively real. We prove the first part of the minor from the testimony of the external senses. From this infallible source we know that many things come into existence which did not exist before, such as plants, animals, and men. But these things which from nonexistence come into existence must have received existence from a being already having actual existence, since they could not have received it from themselves or from nothing, because in either case there would be a violation of the principle of contradiction. But a being which receives existence is a true effect of a real cause.

The second part of the minor is proved from the fact that the connection between cause and effect is often immediately evident. There are of course some cases in which it is difficult to distinguish between a cause and a condition, but there are also many in which the causal connection is obvious. In the great majority of cases it can be discerned readily enough. No sensible man can fail to see the difference between a causal connection and a mere succession of events, although it is true that occasionally we hesitate to assert such a connection because of lack of evidence or erroneously assert it when there is no sufficient evidence for its existence.

Let us examine some of the arguments, or rather assumptions, of the adversaries of efficient causality. As is usual in the case of skeptics, these arguments proceed from the particular to the universal. They maintain that because some have erroneously ascribed causality to certain beings in cases where it did not exist, no one has certainty that there is any such thing as a causal connection. According to them all we can perceive are phenomena which occur in some cases in invariable sequence. This invariable sequence we assume to be a causal connection from a habit of the mind of associating such events within itself. There is, however, no such association in reality except that one event follows the other.

Such a doctrine would evidently make fools of all men. We are all accused of not knowing the difference between the night following the day and the destruction of a city following the dropping of an atomic bomb. According to the phenomenalists both are cases of one thing following another, and there is no difference between them. When we consider the dropping of the bomb as the cause and the destruction of the city as the effect we are adding something to the facts; we just imagine that one was the reason for the occurrence of the other.

The truth of course is that a sequence might be invariable, such as the succession of day and night, and yet no reasonable person would consider that there was a causal connection; while another event might be one that happens but seldom and in a very variable manner, and we would still be sure that it was the result of a certain action. The assertion by the phenomenalists that we obtain our concept of cause and effect from the observation of an event that occurs frequently after another event through the mental habit of association of ideas is contrary to experience and sound common sense. We judge that there is a causal connection even in single cases. What a travesty on justice it would be if the police and the prosecutor had to wait for a man's hundredth murder before accusing him of crime! A city is bombed only once, a ship goes down only once, a man is killed only once, and we do not hesitate to assign the cause of each of these events if we see it in operation.

Even in difficult cases we are able to distinguish between causes and conditions. In the case of seeing, for instance, we know that light is an absolutely necessary condition. In darkness all objects except those that are phosphorescent are invisible. Light, then, is an ordinary antecedent of the vision of objects. Nevertheless, we do not judge light to be the cause of vision, as we should according to the phenomenalist doctrine; but we recognize it as a condition without which vision is impossible, a condition *sine qua non*. The cause we know to be the operative potency of the living being. And so in other cases we distinguish between an active influence (a cause) and a necessary requirement (a condition). Mere sequence, no matter how frequent and invariable, is not the reason why we uphold the validity of the concept of efficient causality. The facts themselves compel the mind to judge that such a relationship exists.

SUMMARY OF CHAPTER XVI

1 **The principle of causality.** It is expressed thus: Whatever passes from a state of nonexistence into a state of existence must have an efficient cause for its existence. The principle of causality is an obvious sequence of the principle of sufficient reason and is therefore analytical and absolutely certain. The new being gets its existence either from itself or from another being. But it cannot be from itself because in that case it would have to act before it existed, which is obviously impossible and contradictory. Hence it must be from another being which produces it. This is its efficient cause.

2 **A misunderstanding corrected.** Modern scientists speak of a principle of causality, but their meaning is something entirely different from that of Aristotle. When a future event can be predicted with absolute certainty from a given set of facts, they call this set of facts the cause of the future event. Their reasoning is from cause to effect. The reasoning in the traditional principle of causality proceeds from effect to cause: there is nothing without a sufficient cause. The principle set forth by scientists should rather be called a principle of predictability or of necessary causation.

3 **Some axioms on efficient causation.** Action follows being—*Operari sequitur esse.* There must be a proportion between cause and effect: *Nemo dat quod non habet*—No one gives what he does not have. Every agent produces something similar to itself, that is, according to its nature—*Omne agens agit simile sibi.*

4 **Cause, condition, occasion.** A cause is that which exerts a positive influence on the production of a thing. A condition is something that is required in order that an efficient cause can act but which does not contribute any positive influence toward the production of the effect. An occasion is a circumstance which affords the efficient cause a better opportunity to act. Neither conditions nor occasions exercise causality; they are only requirements for it or helps to it.

5 **Kinds of efficient causality.** A first cause is one whose causality is absolutely independent of any other cause. This can be only the infinite cause, God. A second cause is one whose causality is dependent on some other cause. All finite causes are second causes.

A physical cause is one which produces an effect by its own action. A moral cause is one which induces a free agent to act.

A principal cause is an efficient cause which produces an effect by virtue of its own power. An instrumental cause is an efficient cause which produces an effect by virtue of the power of a principal cause.

6 **Adversaries of efficient causality.** Phenomenalists deny the existence of efficient causes. They say that we can know only the invariable sequence of events in time and space. Kant held that causality was an *a-priori* mental form, telling us nothing about things in themselves. Occasionalists assert that God is the only source of activity; the activity of creatures is only an appearance.

7 **Proof of efficient causality.** The first proof is from the testimony of consciousness, which tells us that we are true causes of our own acts of mind and body. The second is from external experience, by which we are assured of the production of some beings by other beings. This judgment of course is a judgment of the intellect, but it is forced

upon us by the external facts; and the denial of its truth would be universal skepticism. The assertion that we do not know the difference between invariable sequence and true causation, which is made by the phenomenalists, would make fools of the human race. We judge of causality even in single cases and when the sequence is by no means invariable. We distinguish clearly between causes and conditions, even though there are some cases where there is real difficulty.

CHAPTER XVII

FINAL CAUSES AND THE ORDER OF THE UNIVERSE

WE have already given a preliminary account of the concept of final cause. This final chapter is devoted to a more detailed treatment of the same problem, which is a serious and important one. In addition to all the schools of thought mentioned as adversaries of efficient causality and of the notion of cause in general, there are also opposed to us in the matter of final causality agnostics, positivists, and empiricists. Materialists in general, following the doctrine of mechanism, deny the existence of final causes. The mechanical explanation of the universe, with its theory that all nature consists of homogeneous matter endowed with local motion and that nothing else is required to explain the universe, would obviously repudiate the notion of finality or purpose on the part even of intellectually conscious beings. According to the mechanists there is nowhere in nature any activity which requires any directive principle or shows any evidence of design or purpose. This is also the explanation given by the old Greek atomists whom Aristotle refuted more than two thousand years ago.

The theory of Aristotle and the scholastics gives a purposive or teleological explanation of the universe, one which insists on the existence of final causality or teleology. To the problem as expressed in the well-known question, Do birds fly because they have wings or do they have wings so that they may fly? we answer without hesitation that they do both. They fly because they have wings (efficient causality), and they have wings so that they may fly (final causality or purposefulness). Efficient causes explain the course of nature, but they do not explain why nature takes that course.

Kinds of final causes

There are many different divisions of final cause, but only a few need be considered here. The first division is into intrinsic and extrinsic final causes. The causality of a final cause is said to be *extrinsic* when it is impressed upon a being by some outside directive force. The concept of final causality implies acting for a purpose, with a plan or design for the attainment of some object desired. There must be, then, adaptation of means to ends in the created world if we are to say that it has finality. That there is such adaptation is one of the most common observations of mankind. To quote the famous "Letter of Obedience" of St. Ignatius:

> And this kind of procedure the Divine Providence uses, in disposing all things sweetly, and bringing them to their

appointed ends, the lowest by the middlemost, and the middlemost by the highest. Whence also flows that subordination in Angels of one hierarchy towards another, and that perfect harmony of the celestial bodies and all things which are moved, each in its own determined place and position; whose revolutions and motions proceed orderly from one supreme mover by degrees unto the lowest. The same we see upon earth, as well as in all well-ordered commonwealths, as most of all in the Ecclesiastical Hierarchy, whose members and functions are all derived from one general Vicar of Christ our Lord.[1]

It is the general opinion of men that the things of the universe are useful to one another and are constituted and disposed as if they had been chosen to suit one another, to fit together in mutual relationships of control and subordination so that they work out a plan for the order of the universe. There are innumerable instances of this suitability and adaptation, such as the equilibrium of forces which insures the regular motion of the heavenly bodies which so impressed St. Ignatius, the exact mixture of gases which makes our atmosphere suitable for organic life, the distance and relative positions of the sun and the earth which regulate the climatic conditions necessary for life, the graded hierarchy of living species and the interdependence of plants and animals, and finally the obvious ordination of all lower species for the good of man. This suitability of things relative to one another and this harmony between one creature and another are examples of the extrinsic finality by which the Creator provides for and governs the universe He has called into being.

[1] *Rules of the Society of Jesus,* pp. 65-66. Roehampton: Ex Typographia Manresana, 1926.

The causality of a final cause is said to be *intrinsic* if the action is the result of a being's natural tendencies. Thus we hold that in addition to the extrinsic finality which is impressed on a being from without, it also possesses an intrinsic principle of finality by which its nature directs its activities toward the realization of a good proper to that nature and constituting its intrinsic end or purpose. Accordingly, each being tends to its own proper perfection by its own natural activities at the same time that they all are ordained to an extrinsic purpose which consists in the order and harmony of the whole universe. Thus extrinsic and relative finality ordains that all shall cooperate to constitute a cosmos, a realm of order and beauty, while intrinsic and absolute finality operates so that each creature by a law of its being works toward the realization of a good which is a perfection of its own nature.

An example of this intrinsic finality would be the development of the acorn into the oak which is really in it potentially. The acorn will not develop into an elm, a maple, or a spruce, but only into an oak tree. There is a natural tendency present in the germ plasm of the organic being to develop into a certain specific type, and into that type only, with a regularity and uniformity which give order to the universe. This is true of the whole of organic nature and is especially noteworthy in the human embryo. The fertilized ovum, a simple union of two cells, grows into the marvelously complex human structure with all its intricate organic parts, each in itself adapted to its proper function and to the good of the whole individual. This it does by its own nature by means of an intrinsic tendency present in the cell itself which is the active agent in the production of the complete human being.

Another division of final cause is that into the end of the work and the end of the workman (*finis operis* and *finis operantis*). The end of the work is that to which the being is directed by its very nature, which is therefore intrinsic to itself. The end of the workman is that which the agent himself has in mind in producing the work. These purposes may coincide in a given case, but they need not necessarily do so. For instance, the end of the work of a clock is to tell time, but the end of the man who makes the clock may be to make money or to produce a masterpiece of his art for his own satisfaction.

Proof of the existence of final causes

Unless we wish to deny the clear testimony of our consciousness, we must admit the existence of final causality in intellectual beings. We know that in all our actions we seek a certain good, that we have one or several ends in view by whose desirability we are first attracted and then urged to choose and carry out means for effecting or obtaining this good which the will has chosen as the end or purpose of our actions and desires. It is evident, therefore, that the end or purpose, the good desired, does actually influence the production of our desires and actions and the use of the means which we take to reach their goal. But this is the same as saying that the end or good is a real cause of all that necessarily goes before its actual attainment. Final causality, then, is a fact of rational life—so much so that it is regarded as a sign of loss of reason when a man acts without a rational motive and at variance with the usual purposes of human activity.

From human activity we can argue by analogy to the existence of final causality in brute animals. How similar those actions are in many cases! Whoever has watched a cat lie in wait for a mouse or a bird, or has seen one train its young to do the same thing, must be convinced that the animal is acting with a well-defined purpose. Consider the means they use to protect and preserve their lives, to propagate their kind, and to train their young. Could there be clearer evidence that they are influenced by the good they apprehend and desire?

And, finally, in the domain of plant life and inorganic nature we observe the influence of final causality. Inorganic beings are governed by natural and necessary laws to which they are subject at all times. Chemical affinity is an example of an attraction existing between different elements, and it controls the actions of those elements in many chemical changes. This affinity is a law of physical nature, and is therefore the result of the intrinsic tendencies of the nature of the being itself. Chemical affinity does not produce occasional and haphazard results, but rather effects which are constant, uniform, and mutually useful—effects which help to reproduce and maintain the cosmos which is the universe.

The order of the universe

Aristotle and the scholastics understood the term *nature* to mean the essence of an agent considered as the principle of its activities, determining the direction of those activities, and therefore as the ultimate goal and final cause of those activities. Such is the teleological conception of the nature of the individual agencies constituting the universe. The proof of the doctrine that the beings in the physical universe act under the influence of ends or purposes, that they thereby realize their individual development and maintain the order and harmony of the world, and that by so doing they reveal the overall influence of intelligent purpose, is the fact that their activities are regular, uniform, and productive of order; in other words, that they are regulated by laws, the laws of physical nature.

The mechanistic explanation, on the other hand, does not admit the existence in physical agencies of any law that would indicate the presence of a natural inclination toward a good or that would in any way imply intelligence, design, or purpose. Mechanists assert, as we have seen before, that all physical phenomena are reducible to mechanical motions of inert atoms or particles of matter in space which are, therefore, entirely indifferent to any particular form of activity. This school of thought accordingly can give no rational explanation of the actual order and course of the universe. With both these factors entirely indifferent, it might still be possible to explain order and design on the basis of extrinsic finality; but mechanism will not admit even extrinsic finality. It will not admit any evidence of a guiding intelligence working out a plan or design for any rational purpose. The only account, then, that mechanists can give of the world is that offered by the old Greek atomists: the universe is ruled by blind chance, fate, or accident. But this is no answer to the problem of order, but rather a denial or avoidance of the difficulty.

To understand the relationship between that problem and the existence of final causes, it will be of help to indicate briefly what order involves. Order implies a principle of unity among many things. St. Thomas defines order as *recta ratio rerum ad finem*—the due adaptation of means to an end. It is evident, then, that the unifying principle of order is the influence of the end, or purpose, or final cause. It is in fact impossible to understand order except as resulting from final causes. And this in turn necessitates the existence of intelligent purpose and intelligent will. Reason rejects an explanation of the order of the universe which supposes a chance arrangement of indifferent and aimless physical constituents. The opinion of Aristotle is given in the second book of the *Physics:*

> In general the theory of chance as the dominant factor in the universe does away with the whole order of Nature, and indeed with Nature's self. For natural things are exactly those which do move continuously, in virtue of a principle inherent in themselves toward a determined goal; and the final development which results from any one such principle is not identical for any two species, nor yet is it any random result: but in each there is always a tendency toward an identical result if nothing interferes with the process. A desirable result and the means to it may also be produced by chance, as for instance we say it was "by luck" that the stranger came and ransomed the prisoner before he left, where the ransoming is done as if the man had come for that purpose, though in fact he did not. In this case the desirable result is incidental; for, as we have explained, chance is an incidental cause. But when the desirable result

is effected invariably or normally, it is not an incidental or chance occurrence; and in the course of Nature the result always is achieved invariably or normally if nothing hinders. It is absurd to suppose that there is no purpose because in Nature we can never detect the moving power in the act of deliberating. . . . That Nature is the cause, then, and a goal-directed cause, is above dispute.[2]

Nature indeed has no intelligence of its own, and therefore cannot choose the goal of its action, the good which is the end or purpose of its striving. Nevertheless, intelligence there must be if nature is a "goal-directed cause" tending toward the actualization of its purpose according to definite laws. Therefore the presence of a goal or purpose in nature requires the existence of a supreme intelligence outside of and above nature. Further discussion of this point is reserved for natural theology.

The meaning of chance

We have already spoken of chance or accident several times when contrasting it with final causality. When people speak of chance they ordinarily mean any event which happens without being intended, in which there is no purpose or final cause on the part of the agent. Chance results, however, must not be understood as occurring without a cause. This would be impossible, a violation of the principle of causality. Adequate efficient and other causality exists; but the agent did not intend this particular result, and therefore it is said to have happened by accident.

[2] *Physics,* Bk. 2, Chap. 8, 199, b, 15-30.

Aristotle's definition of chance, or luck, or accident (all these expressions mean the same thing) is penetrating and enlightening:

> the production of some significant result by a cause that took its place in the causal chain incidentally, and without the result in question being contemplated. . . . Clearly, then, luck itself, regarded as a cause, is the name we give to causation which incidentally inheres in deliberately purposeful action taken with respect to some other end but leading to the event we call fortunate or unfortunate.[3]

Let us consider the example of a very common accident indeed, the crash of two automobiles. Both drivers are speeding along, each having his own particular objective and employing the proper means to get there. Neither driver foresees that, driving as they are now and under the present conditions, their cars will meet at right angles at the next intersection. The two sets of efficient causes are both purposeful, but their conjuncture at that particular time is only incidental and perhaps beyond their knowledge and control.

In accidental occurrences, therefore, there are two distinct efficient causes, each intending a definite result, but the coincidence of these separate agents is not intended and not desired. In that consists the element of chance or luck, since no principle regulates or controls the meeting of these independent actions. They are incidental results of other actions which are known and willed. These incidental and accidental results are therefore beyond the knowledge and the power of any finite being. Their characteristic marks are those of inconstancy and irregularity,

[3] *Physics,* Bk. 2, Chap. 5, 196, b, 30; 197, a, 5.

whereas actions which are governed by final causes according to physical laws occur regularly and constantly in nature, and therefore cannot be the result of chance or accident.

Aristotle does not carry his analysis of chance in the *Physics* to its logical conclusion. There must be an ultimate explanation of such accidental encounters in the universe, of such lack of control of individual phenomena. Such chance effects are not entirely purposeless nor wholly unintended. They are part of the general plan as known and willed by the author of nature, the governor of the universe. They are known to His intelligence and willed by His providence. For the infinite there can be no such thing as chance. All such events are foreseen and willed by Him and made to take their proper place in that universal order which is heaven's first law. It is only in relation to finite agencies and to finite intelligence that such phenomena can be called the result of chance.

Axioms concerning final causes

The end or purpose is first in the order of causation and nobler than the other kinds of causes—Finis in ordine causarum est prima et praestantior ceteris causarum speciebus. As St. Thomas says, quoting Aristotle, the purpose is *quodammodo causa aliarum causarum,* the cause of all the other causes. This is readily seen; for if the purpose, which is the first in order of causes, is withdrawn, the efficient cause will have no motive for action and therefore will not produce anything. If nothing is produced, then neither is there any formal or material cause. The purpose also determines the use of the means or instrumental cause. Thus all the other causes are for the sake of the end, but the final cause is the good sought for its own sake.

The end is first in intention, last in execution—Finis est prima in intentione, ultima in executione. The purpose is the good to be attained, the result to be achieved in the future by the means, the productive action which begins in the present. The action is then determined from the beginning by the good which is desired as the end, but this good is achieved only after the use of proper means. This axiom does not violate the principle of contradiction, for the end is not first and last under the same aspect.

Who intends the end, must intend the means—Qui vult finem, velle debet media. Whoever has an end in mind must rationally employ some means to attain it; otherwise there is no efficacious intention. It follows that whoever employs certain means to attain his purpose is responsible for the willing of the means as well as for the willing of the end. If, then, those means are morally evil, he is responsible for the moral evil. Hence the axiom, important for the science of ethics, *The end does not justify the means.* No morally evil action may be done, no matter how much goodness there may be in the end or purpose.

There must be a proportion between the means and the end—Debet esse proportio inter medium et finem. Almost every language has an old adage which is a variation of this axiom. One does not kill a fly with an ax nor burn down his house because his fingers are frostbitten. Common sense and prudence would demand that we choose means to our ends which are neither too great nor too puny. It is the mistake of the sinner to strive after what is worthless with extraordinary care and diligence, and of the foolish to expect great results from slight effort or labor.

The reality of final causes

The question arises as to how a final cause can exercise any causality or be a real cause when it is evident from its nature that it does not exist in the beginning but only after its production by proper means. According to the definition, a cause is something that exercises a positive influence on the production of a thing. But how can anything exercise a positive influence when it does not really exist? It seems impossible that any such influence could be exercised by a nonexistent being. For example, an artist intends to make a statue of Venus. The statue, then, is the final cause. But as yet it is only a dream, an idea. The marble may be at hand, but it will take years to carve the statue. How, then, can the statue exercise any causality when it is not an existing reality?

The answer is simple. The end or purpose does not exist in the physical order, but it has another kind of reality, the reality of a possible being in the metaphysical order, which is the second kind of reality, of real being. Because it is real it can and does influence other beings. As some philosophers say, it exists in the intentional order, by which they mean the same thing, as is obvious if we recall that there are two kinds of metaphysical being, objective and subjective. Subjective metaphysical being exists in the mind as a representation; objective metaphysical being is a reality of the potential order, the thing which can be thought of or represented. The lack of physical existence is no bar to the exercise of causality. It is, in fact, the very reason why causality is set in motion—to bring into the realm of physical things those dreams and hopes and plans which obviously are not nothing, but are real beings waiting to be actualized by the creative influence of God and man, the one as first cause and the other as second cause.

Final causation is thus a reality in nature precisely because it is a possible, an essence, a metaphysical being which has its reality in the mind of the agent and in the mind of God subjectively, and objectively as a real being in itself *(in se ipso)*. And so we end where we began, with the notion that real being is of two kinds, actual and possible or physical and metaphysical. This idea constitutes not only the beginning and the end of metaphysics, but also a good deal of what comes in between.

SUMMARY OF CHAPTER XVII

1 **Kinds of final causes.** As opposed to almost all modern philosophy, the doctrine of Aristotle insists on the existence of final causes (teleology). The adversaries of the doctrine are those mentioned in the preceding chapter plus materialists, agnostics, positivists, and empiricists.

Final causes may be divided in several ways. One division is into extrinsic and intrinsic causes. Final causality is extrinsic when it is impressed on the being from without by some directive force. Extrinsic causality operates so that all beings shall constitute a cosmos, a universe of order and beauty. Final causality is said to be intrinsic when the action is the result of the being's natural tendencies. Each being possesses a nature which by an intrinsic principle directs its activities toward a good proper to that nature and constituting its intrinsic end or purpose.

Final causes are also divided into the end of the work and the end of the workman *(finis operis* and *finis operantis)*. The end of the work is that which is intrinsic and natural to an object. The end of the workman is the intention which the agent has in producing the work.

2 **Proof of the existence of final causes.** From the testimony of consciousness we are certain that in all our actions we seek a certain good and intend the means to obtain it; but this is to act for a final cause. We can argue to a similar conclusion about brute animals from analogy. It is obvious that they know and desire the good they seek according to their nature. Physical laws such as chemical affinity prove the same thing for plants and inorganic nature.

3 **The order of the universe.** Aristotle and the scholastics had a teleological conception of the universe—the nature of a being determines its activities and directs it to its ultimate goal and final cause. Mechanists, on the other hand, deny final causality and insist that all physical phenomena are reducible to mechanical motions of inert and homogeneous particles of matter entirely indifferent to any form of activity. But there is order in the universe, and order cannot be understood except as resulting from final causes. Aristotle's proof of this is that the results are regular and uniform according to physical laws.

4 **The meaning of chance.** Aristotle defines chance as "the production of some significant result by a cause that took its place in the causal chain incidentally, and without the result in question being contemplated." There are two effi-

cient causes at work, each having its own end but neither intending their conjuncture. Accidental results do not occur with the constancy and regularity of purposeful results under physical laws, and that is the difference between chance and final causality. Chance results are not entirely without control. There is no such thing as chance to infinite intelligence and infinite providence. All events contribute to the order of the universe which He has established.

5 **Axioms concerning final causes.** The end or purpose is first in the order of causation and nobler than the other causes. The end is first in intention, last in execution. Who intends the end must intend the means. There must be a proportion between the means and the end.

6 **The reality of final causes.** The question arises as to how a final cause can exert any causality, any positive influence, when it does not exist. The answer is that it does not have physical reality but that it does have metaphysical reality, and this enables it to influence the effect. It has existence as a subjective or intentional metaphysical being and has a reality of its own in the metaphysical order.

ABSTRACTION. A process in which the mind fixes its attention upon one characteristic of a thing or upon one element common to many things, excluding other elements which are joined to it in the real order. *See also* Precision.

ACCIDENT. A being whose nature it is to exist in another as in a subject.

Absolute accident. An accident which confers a real perfection upon its subject.

Extrinsic accident. An accident which does not affect the being of its subject, but modifies the subject indirectly and externally.

Intrinsic accident. An accident which affects the being of its subject in some manner.

Modal accident. The definite disposition or determination of an indifferent and determinable accidental being in such a manner that it does not confer any positive and new entity upon the substance.

Relative accident. An accident that has its being in a subject because of its reference to another being.

ACT. The entity of whatever kind and nature which perfects and determines a thing in its being.

ACTION. The exercise or operation of an operative potency. The production of an effect.

ACTIVITY

Immanent activity. The activity through which a living being perfects itself and makes itself the goal for the acquired actuality or perfection.

Transient activity. Activity which tends to change another object.

AFFECTION. A relatively transient quality which produces, or results from, some accidental sensible alteration.

ALTERATION. The change of a being from one qualitative state to another.

ANNIHILATION. The reduction of an existing being to nonexistence.

ATTRIBUTES, TRANSCENDENTAL. The supreme modes necessarily connected with every being, which are different phases of the being but are not explicitly contained in its concept as such. The transcendental attributes are oneness, truth, and goodness.

AUGMENTATION. A change in a being which brings about an increase in quantity.

BEAUTY. That attribute of a thing in virtue of which the thing pleases when perceived. A blending of the unity, truth, and goodness in a thing, characterized by completeness, proportion, and clarity of presentation in an intellectual sensuous form, so as to produce a disinterested emotional pleasure in a rational perceiver.

BEING. That which exists or can exist; the existible; whatever is not nothing.

Absolute being. A being which can be thought of without reference to another. It is independent of other beings in the order of thought.

Actual being. Anything that really exists at the present moment in the physical order. It may be either spiritual or material.

Contingent being. A being whose nonexistence is possible.

Contraction of being. The reduction or narrowing of the *extension* of being by means of the addition of some element to the *comprehension* of being, thereby including some definite beings and excluding others.

Finite being. A being which is limited in perfection.

Ideal being. Any object insofar as it is known. Ideal being may be either subjective or objective. Subjectively, it is the mental image, the representation; objectively, it is the thing represented, the essence, or objective metaphysical being.

Infinite being. A being which has no limit in its entity or perfection.

Logical being. Anything that has objective being only in the mind.

Necessary being. A being whose nonexistence is impossible.

Possible being. Anything that does not actually exist, but is capable of existence. It has a positive metaphysical reality in itself *(in se ipso)*.

Real being. Anything that has, or can have, existence independently of man's mind.

Relative being. A being which can be thought of only in reference to another.

CAPACITY, NATURAL. A proximate accidental principle of operation which is directed toward a specific operation.

CATEGORY. One of the ten supreme classes of real being; a predicament.

CAUSALITY, PRINCIPLE OF. Whatever passes from a state of nonexistence into a state of existence must have an efficient cause for its existence.

CAUSE. That which in any way whatever exerts a positive influence on the production of a thing.

Efficient cause. That by whose action something is produced.

Final cause. That for the sake of which an efficient cause acts.

First cause. A cause whose causality is absolutely independent of any other cause or being, and on which all other causality depends.

Formal cause. That through which a thing is made to be what it is. Form.

Instrumental cause. An efficient cause which produces an effect in virtue of the power of another cause.

Material cause. That out of which something becomes or is made. Matter.

Moral cause. A cause which inclines a free agent to act.

Physical cause. A cause which produces an effect by its own direct action.

Principal cause. An efficient cause which produces an effect in virtue of its own power.

Secondary cause. A cause whose causality is dependent on some other cause or being.

CHANCE. Causality which results in effects not intended by the agents under these particular circumstances.

CHANGE. The transition from one positive state of being to another.

Principle of change. Whatever changes is changed by another.

COMPOSITION

Objective composition. The union of elements that are objectively different in idea, but really identical in their physical being as things.

Subjective composition. The union of elements which are not objectively different in idea, but merely different in the sense that one idea contains implicitly and vaguely what the other expresses explicitly and determinately; applied only to the composition of being with its divisions.

CONDITION. Something required in order that an efficient cause may act.

CONTRADICTION, PRINCIPLE OF. It is impossible for a thing to be and not to be at the same time and under the same aspect.

CORRUPTION. A substantial change which makes a substance cease to be.

CREATION. The production of a thing from nothing.

DETERMINATIONS, TRANSCENDENTAL. Those primary determinations which constitute the most fundamental distinctions of "being in general" and go beyond all the ordinary classifications of beings.

DIMINUTION. A change in a being which results in a decrease in quantity.

DISTINCTION. The absence of identity between concepts or things.

Formal distinction of Duns Scotus. Same as St. Thomas' logical distinction with a perfect foundation in the thing. Based on an objective essence or an objective metaphysical being.

Logical distinction. The absence of identity between concepts which express the same reality. According to the general opinion, the foundation in reality for the distinction may be either perfect or imperfect. The text proves, however, that the term logical distinction should be confined to one which has a so-called imperfect foundation in reality—that is, *some* foundation.

Major real distinction. The absence of identity between two things that are distinct from each other as entities.

Minor real distinction. The absence of identity between a thing and its mode.

Purely mental distinction. A distinction between concepts having one and the same reality, without any foundation in the object itself for making the distinction.

Real distinction. The absence of identity between beings that differ in their reality, independently of the action of the mind.

EFFECT. That which is produced.

END (PURPOSE; FINAL CAUSE). That for the sake of which an agent or efficient cause acts.

End of the work (act). The purpose to which the act is directed by its very nature.

End of the workman (agent). The purpose which the agent has in performing a particular act.

ERROR. Lack of conformity (disagreement) between intellect and thing. *See also* Falsity.

ESSENCE. The perfection which determines a thing in its species; that which makes a thing to be what it is.

Metaphysical essence. The sum of the various grades of being which constitute a thing as it is considered by the mind.

Physical essence. An essence as it exists concretely in nature, independently of the action of the mind.

EVIL. Something that is unsuitable for a natural tendency or appetency. The privation of a required good.

Moral evil. The privation of the proper relation between a human act and its norm or criterion of morality.

Physical evil. The privation of a physical good.

EXCLUDED MIDDLE, PRINCIPLE OF. A thing either is or is not. Everything must either be or not be. Between *being* and *nonbeing* there is no middle or third thing possible.

EXISTENCE. That state of a being in virtue of which it is present as an actuality and not merely as a possibility, distinct from the mind and, if it be a produced being, distinct from its producing cause.

FALSITY (ERROR). Lack of conformity (disagreement) between intellect and thing.

Logical falsity. Disagreement of the intellect with the thing.

Moral falsity. Disagreement of speech with thought.

Ontological falsity. Disagreement of a thing with the intellect.

FINAL CAUSE. That for the sake of which an agent or efficient cause acts.

Extrinsic final cause. A final cause whose causal action is impressed upon it by some outside directive force.

Intrinsic final cause. A final cause whose action in producing a definite effect is the result of its natural tendencies.

FUTURIBLE. That which might have taken place if circumstances had been otherwise, particularly if the free will had chosen otherwise than it actually did.

GENERATION. A substantial change which brings a new substance into being through the corruption of another.

GOOD. Any reality which suits the nature of the being which strives for it.

Absolute good. Anything which is suitable to a being itself, irrespective of other beings.

Apparent good. Something that is judged to be good for a being, but is actually not good for it.

Moral good. An action which is in conformity with the moral law.

Ontological good. The being or reality of a thing.

Physical good. A good which perfects the nature of a being. It could be either material or immaterial. The soul is a greater physical good than the brain.

Real good. Something that is judged to be good for a being and actually is good for it.

GOODNESS. The suitability of a thing for a natural tendency or appetency.

HABIT. A quality, stable and difficult to remove, disposing a thing well or ill in its being or in its operations.

Operative habit. A stable quality disposing a being ill or well in the operations of its faculties.

HABITUS. The accidental modification of a being resulting from clothing, equipment, physical adjuncts, or environment.

IDENTITY. The sameness of concepts or things.

Accidental logical identity. The logical identity of things based upon the similarity of their accidents.

Essential logical identity. The logical identity of things based upon the sameness of their essence.

Logical identity. The unity (oneness) of things which correspond to the same concept in the mind.

Metaphysical identity. The real identity of a being in such a way that it cannot change in any manner whatsoever.

Moral identity. The real identity of a being in such a way that any change which takes place in its essential nature is successive and gradual.

Physical identity. The real identity of a being in such a way that it does not change in its essential reality.

Principle of identity. Whatever is, is; and whatever is not, is not. Everything is what it is. Everything is its own being. Being is being, and nonbeing is nonbeing.

Real identity. The unity (oneness) of things in themselves.

INCAPACITY. An existing faculty in a weakened or unfit condition.

INDIVIDUALITY. That state of an existing being in virtue of which it is one and not multipliable.

Unity of individuality. The unity of a being which is one in itself and not multipliable.

INDIVIDUATION, PRINCIPLE OF. The principle which makes an existing being to be an individual, so that its nature or essence is incommunicable to others and is restricted to this one.

Principle of absolute individuation. That intrinsic principle which gives the unity of individuality to an existing being.

Principle of relative individuation. The principle which determines the possibility of having a number of individuals of the same species.

MECHANISM. The theory which maintains that the ultimate constituent particles of matter are homogeneous in character and actuated by purely mechanical forces which produce only local movement.

METAPHYSICS. The science of the ultimate principles and properties of real beings.

MOTION, LOCAL. The transition of a thing from one place to another.

NATURE. The essence of a being considered as the ultimate principle of its operations.

NOTHING. The absence of being.

Absolute nothing. The total absence of real being.

Negative nothing. The mere absence in a thing of some kind of being which its nature does not require.

Privative nothing. The absence in a thing of some kind of being with which nature ordinarily endows it.

Relative nothing. The absence of a particular kind of being. Relative nothing may be either negative or privative.

OCCASION. A circumstance or combination of circumstances which affords an opportunity for an efficient cause to act.

ONENESS. That attribute of a being in virtue of which it is undivided in itself and divided from every other being.

PASSION (REACTION). The reception of an action from another.

PHILOSOPHY. The science of things in their ultimate reasons, causes, and principles, acquired by the use of human reason alone.

POSSIBILITY. Objective potency, or the capacity or aptitude of a being for existence.

Extrinsic possibility. The capacity or aptitude of a being for existence in virtue of the existence of an efficient cause capable of producing it.

Intrinsic possibility. The capacity or aptitude of a being for existence in virtue of the compatibility or noncontradiction of its constituent elements.

Moral possibility. The possibility of free agents to do something without grave difficulty.

Physical possibility. The possibility due to the powers of a thing acting according to the laws of nature.

POTENCY. The capacity or aptitude for something.

Objective potency. The capacity of a nonexistent being for existence.

Operative subjective potency. The capacity for doing something.

Receptive subjective potency. The capacity for receiving an act.

Subjective potency. The capacity of something existing for another act or perfection.

PRECISION. A process in which the mind fixes its attention upon one characteristic of a thing or upon one element common to many things, excluding other elements with which it is really identified in the physical order. *See also* Abstraction.

Objective precision. A type of precision in which the ideas drawn out by the abstractive process are objectively different; that is, these ideas have a different comprehension or thought content, so that one does not necessarily include the other (for example, the idea of animal and the idea of rational).

Subjective precision. A type of precision in which the ideas drawn out by the abstractive process are only subjectively different; that is, the ideas mutually include each other implicitly, although they do not expressly mention each other (for example, the ideas of being and substance or accident).

PREDICAMENT. An ultimate and supreme mode of being; a category.

PREMOTION, PHYSICAL. An antecedent physical influence *(praemotio physica)* which, according to Thomists, is required in order that the faculty of a creature may pass from potentiality to actuality.

PRINCIPLE. That from which something proceeds in any manner whatever.

PRINCIPLES, SUPREME, OF BEING. Those highest principles which are immediately derived from the concept of being.

PROPERTIES, TRANSCENDENTAL. The supreme modes or attributes necessarily connected with every being.

PROPERTY. The act or actuality perfecting and determining an essence in such a manner that the entity it gives to the being flows necessarily from its nature, without being strictly a part of the essence.

QUALITY. An absolute accident completing and determining a substance in its being and in its operations.

Affective quality. A relatively permanent quality which produces, or results from, some accidental sensible alteration.

QUANTITY. An attribute of the material element in a being.

QUIDDITY. The "whatness" or essence of a being.

REACTION (PASSION). The reception of an action from another.

RELATION. The bearing (reference, respect, attitude, ordination) of one thing to something else.

Accidental (predicamental) relation. A relation based on an accident as its foundation.

Essential (transcendental) relation. A relation in which the very essence of one thing has a bearing toward something else.

Extremes of relation. The subject and the term of a relation.

Foundation of relation. The reason why one thing is related to another.

Logical relation. A relation that depends solely on the activity of the mind; the foundation for the relation exists only in the mind.

Real relation. A relation which exists between things, independently of the mind and its operations.

SUBSTANCE. A being whose nature it is to exist in itself and which does not need another as a subject of inherence.

Complete substance. A substance whose nature demands no further union with a substantial coprinciple.

Composite substance. A substance consisting of incomplete substantial parts, entitatively distinct and so joined that their union results in a single, unified nature.

Incomplete substance. A substance whose nature is ordained to be united with a substantial coprinciple.

Primary substance. Any individual, concrete substantial being.

Secondary substance. Any generic or specific substance. A universal concept or idea.

Simple substance. A substance which is not composed of any parts into which it could be divided.

SUFFICIENT REASON, PRINCIPLE OF. Everything must have a reason for its being or existence.

TELEOLOGY. The tendency of efficient causes to realize definite results through their action.

TERM

Analogous term. A term predicated of different things in a sense partly the same and partly different.

Equivocal term. A term predicated of several things in an entirely different sense.

Univocal term. A term predicated of several things in exactly the same sense.

TERMINUS

Terminus a quo. The starting point from which something begins.

Terminus ad quem. The goal toward which something proceeds.

TRANSCENDENTAL. That which is outside all ordinary classifications and categories of being and which can be applied to every being of whatever kind.

TRUTH. Conformity (agreement) between intellect and thing.

Logical truth. Agreement of the intellect with the thing.

Moral truth. Agreement of speech with thought.

Ontological (metaphysical) truth. The agreement of a being with the intellect.

UNITY. That mode or attribute of a being in virtue of which it is undivided in itself and, as a consequence, divided from every other being.

Logical unity. The indivision of a universal idea (class) considered as a conceptual whole of which the members are parts.

Predicamental unity. A unit considered as a standard for measuring mathematical or numerical quantity.

Real unity. The indivision of a thing in its being, independently of the mind.

Unity of composition. The kind of unity belonging to a compound being when it is not actually divided into the real parts of which it is composed.

Unity of simplicity. The kind of unity belonging to a being that does not consist of any parts into which it could be divided.

WHEN. Situation in time.

WHERE. Position in space.

BIBLIOGRAPHY

Albert the Great. *Opera omnia.* 38 vols. Paris: 1890-1899.

Anderson, James F. *Introduction to the Metaphysics of St. Thomas Aquinas.* Chicago: Henry Regnery Company, 1953.

Aristotle. *Works of Aristotle,* edited by W. D. Ross. 12 vols. Oxford: Clarendon Press, 1908-1952.

Balmes, James. *Fundamental Philosophy,* translated by Henry F. Brownson. 2 vols. New York: D. and J. Sadlier and Company, 1858.

Bandas, Rudolph G. *Contemporary Philosophy and Thomistic Principles.* Milwaukee: Bruce Publishing Company, 1932.

Baschab, Charles R. *Manual of Neo-Scholastic Philosophy.* St. Louis: B. Herder Book Company, 1923.

Bittle, Celestine N. *Domain of Being: Ontology.* Milwaukee: Bruce Publishing Company, 1939.

Boedder, Bernard. *Natural Theology.* New York: Longmans, Green and Company, 1927.

Bonaventure, St. *Opera omnia.* 10 vols. Quaracchi: 1882-1902.

Bowne, Borden P. *Metaphysics.* New York: American Book Company, 1898.

Bradley, F. H. *Appearance and Reality.* New York: The Macmillan Company, 1902.

——— *Essays on Truth and Reality.* New York: Oxford University Press, 1914.

Burtt, E. A. *Metaphysical Foundation of Modern Physical Science.* New York: Harcourt, Brace and Company, 1925.

Carr, H. W. *Philosophy of Change.* New York: The Macmillan Company, 1914.

Coffey, P. *Ontology.* New York: Longmans, Green and Company, 1914.

De Maria, Michael. *Philosophia peripatetico-scholastica.* 3 vols. Rome: Philip Cuggiani, 1904.

Descoqs, P. *Institutiones metaphysicae generalis.* Paris: Gabriel Beauchesne, 1925.

Dulles, A. R., and others. *Introductory Metaphysics.* New York: Sheed and Ward, 1955.

Esser, Gerard. *Metaphysica generalis.* Techny: 1933.

Felkin, Fred W. *Workbook of Metaphysics.* London: Oxford University Press, 1932.

Frick, Charles. *Logic.* Fribourg: Herder, 1934.

——— *Ontology.* Fribourg: Herder, 1934.

Garrigou-Lagrange, Reginald. *Le realisme du principe de finalité.* Paris: Desclee De Brouwer, 1932.

Geyser, Joseph. *Einige Hauptprobleme der Metaphysic.* Fribourg: Herder, 1923.

Gilson, Etienne. *Being and Some Philosophers,* second edition. Toronto: Pontifical Institute of Mediaeval Studies, 1952.

——— *Philosophy of St. Thomas Aquinas,* translated by Edward Bullough. St. Louis: B. Herder Book Company, 1930.

Gredt, Joseph. *Elementa philosophiae Aristotelico-Thomisticae.* 2 vols. St. Louis: B. Herder Book Company, 1931.

Gutberlet, C. *Allgemeine Metaphysic.* Münster: Theissingsche Buchhandlung, 1906.

Haldane, Richard Burdon. *Pathway to Reality.* New York: E. P. Dutton and Company, 1926.

Harper, Thomas. *Metaphysics of the School.* 3 vols. New York: Longmans, Green and Company, 1940.

Harris, C. R. S. *Duns Scotus.* 2 vols. Oxford: Clarendon Press, 1927.

Hart, Charles A., editor. *Aspects of the New Scholastic Philosophy.* New York: Benziger Brothers, 1932.

Hawkins, D. J. B. *Being and Becoming.* New York: Sheed and Ward, 1954.

Hickey, J. S. *Summula philosophiae scholasticae.* 3 vols. St. Louis: B. Herder Book Company, 1917.

Hontheim, Joseph. *Theodicea, sive theologia naturalis.* Fribourg: Herder and Company, 1926.

Joyce, George H. *Principles of Natural Theology.* New York: Longmans, Green and Company, 1923.

Kallen, H. M., and Hook, Sidney, editors. *American Philosophy Today and Tomorrow.* New York: Lee Furman, 1935.

Klubertanz, George P. *Introduction to the Philosophy of Being.* New York: Appleton-Century-Crofts, 1955.

Koren, Henry J. *Introduction to the Science of Metaphysics.* St. Louis: B. Herder Book Company, 1955.

Lange, Frederick A. *History of Materialism,* translated by Ernest C. Thomas. New York: Harcourt, Brace and Company, 1925.

Lortie, Stanislaus. *Elementa philosophiae Christianae.* Quebec: L'Action Sociale, 1921.

McCormick, John F. *Scholastic Metaphysics.* Chicago: Loyola University Press, 1928.

Maritain, Jacques. *Introduction to Philosophy,* translated by E. I. Watkin. New York: Sheed and Ward, 1930.

——— *Preface to Metaphysics.* New York: Sheed and Ward, 1948.

Mercier, D. Cardinal. *Manual of Modern Scholastic Philosophy,* translated by T. L. Parker and S. A. Parker, second edition. 2 vols. London: Kegan Paul, Trench, Trubner and Company; St. Louis: B. Herder Book Company, 1921.

——— *Métaphysique générale.* Louvain: Institut Superieur de Philosophie, 1910.

Miltner, Charles C. *Introduction to Metaphysics.* New York: The Macmillan Company, 1930.

Morgan, C. Lloyd. *Emergent Evolution.* New York: Henry Holt and Company, 1923.

Muirhead, J. H., editor. *Contemporary British Philosophy,* First Series. New York: The Macmillan Company, 1924.

——— *Contemporary British Philosophy,* Second Series. New York: The Macmillan Company, 1926.

Osgniach, A. J. *Analysis of Objects.* New York: Joseph F. Wagner, 1938.

Perry, Ralph Barton. *Present Philosophical Tendencies.* New York: Longmans, Green and Company, 1912.

Pesch, Tilmann. *Institutiones logicales.* Fribourg: Herder and Company, 1888.

Phelan, Gerald B. *Saint Thomas and Analogy* (Aquinas Lecture, 1941). Milwaukee: Marquette University Press, 1941.

Phillips, R. P. *Modern Thomistic Philosophy.* 2 vols. London: Burns Oates and Washbourne, 1934-1935.

Planck, Max. *Philosophy of Physics,* translated by W. H. Johnston. New York: W. W. Norton and Company, 1936.

——— *Where Is Science Going?* translated by James Murphy. New York: W. W. Norton and Company, 1932.

Plato. *Plato,* translated by H. N. Fowler and W. R. M. Lamb. 12 vols. Cambridge: Harvard University Press, 1914-1934.

Pontifex, Mark, and Trethowan, Illtyd. *Meaning of Existence.* London: Longmans, Green and Company, 1953.

Raeymaeker, Louis de. *Philosophy of Being,* translated by Edmund H. Ziegelmeyer. St. Louis: B. Herder Book Company, 1954.

Renard, Henri. *Philosophy of Being,* second edition. Milwaukee: Bruce Publishing Company, 1948.

Rickaby, John. *General Metaphysics.* New York: Longmans, Green and Company, 1921.

Robinson, Daniel S., compiler. *Anthology of Modern Philosophy.* New York: Thomas Y. Crowell Company, 1931.

———, compiler. *Anthology of Recent Philosophy.* New York: Thomas Y. Crowell Company, 1929.

——— *Introduction to Living Philosophy*. New York: Thomas Y. Crowell Company, 1932.

Ryan, James H. *Introduction to Philosophy*. New York: The Macmillan Company, 1924.

Salmon, Elizabeth G. *The Good in Existential Metaphysics*. Milwaukee: Marquette University Press, 1953.

Shallo, Michael W. *Lessons in Scholastic Philosophy*. Philadelphia: Peter Rielly Company, 1934.

Shea, Bernard V. *Notes on the Science of Ontology*. Worcester: Holy Cross College Press, 1951.

Sheen, Fulton J. *Philosophy of Science*. Milwaukee: Bruce Publishing Company, 1934.

Shircel, Cyril Louis. *Univocity of the Concept of Being in the Philosophy of John Duns Scotus*. Washington: Catholic University of America, 1942.

Suarez, Francis. *Disputationes metaphysicae*. Paris: L. Vives, 1877.

——— *On the Various Kinds of Distinctions (Disputationes metaphysicae, disp. 7)*, translated by Cyril Vollert. Milwaukee: Marquette University Press, 1947.

Taylor, A. E. *Elements of Metaphysics*. London: Methuen and Company, 1946.

Thomas Aquinas, St. *On Being and Essence,* translated by Armand Maurer. Toronto: Pontifical Institute of Mediaeval Studies, 1948.

——— *Summa contra gentiles,* translated by Fathers of the English Dominican Province. 5 vols. London: Burns Oates and Washbourne, 1924-1929.

——— *Summa theologica,* translated by Fathers of the English Dominican Province. 3 vols. New York: Benziger Brothers, 1947-1948.

Tongiorgi, Salvator. *Institutiones philosophicae*. Paris: Lecoffre Son and Associates, 1878.

Urban, Wilbur M. *The Intelligible World*. New York: The Macmillan Company, 1939.

Urráburu, Juan José. *Institutiones philosophicae*. Valladolid: Cuesta, 1890-1900.

Van Steenberghen, F. *Ontology*. New York: Joseph F. Wagner, 1952.

Walshe, T. J. *Quest of Reality*. St. Louis: B. Herder Book Company, 1933.

Ward, Leo R. *Values and Reality*. New York: Sheed and Ward, 1935.

Whitehead, Alfred North. *Process and Reality*. New York: The Macmillan Company, 1929.

Wild, John. *Introduction to Realistic Philosophy*. New York: Harper and Brothers, 1948.

——— *Return to Reason*. Chicago: Henry Regnery Company, 1953.

DeWulf, Maurice. *History of Medieval Philosophy,* translated by Ernest C. Messenger. New York: Dover, 1952.

——— *Scholasticism Old and New,* translated by P. Coffey. New York: Benziger Brothers, 1907.

Zybura, J. S. *Present-Day Thinkers and the New Scholasticism*. St. Louis: B. Herder Book Company, 1926.

INDEX

Index

Index